Transsexuality and the Art of Transitioning

Transsexuality and the Art of Transitioning: A Lacanian approach presents a startling new way to consider psychoanalytic dilemmas of sexual difference and gender through the meeting of arts and the clinic. Informed by a Lacanian perspective that locates transsexuality in the intermediate space between the clinic and culture, Oren Gozlan joins current conversations around the question of sexual difference with the insistence that identity never fully expresses sexuality and, as such, cannot be replaced by gender.

The book goes beyond the idea of gender as an experience that gives rise to multiple identities and instead considers identity as split from the outset. This view transforms transsexuality into a particular psychic position, able to encounter the paradoxes of transitional experience and the valence of phantasy and affect that accompany aesthetic conflicts over the nature of beauty and being. Gozlan brings readers into the enigmatic qualities of representation as desire for completion and transformation through notions of tension, difference and aesthetics, through examining the artwork of Anish Kapoor and Louise Bourgeois and the role played by confusion in the aesthetics of transformation in literature and memoir. Fundamentally, this work understands transsexuality as a creative act, rich with desire and danger, in which thinking of the transsexual body as both an analytic and a subjective object helps us to reveal the creativity of sexuality.

Ideal for psychoanalysts, psychologists, psychiatrists and social workers as well as students of psychoanalysis, cultural studies, literature studies and philosophy, *Transsexuality and the Art of Transitioning* offers a unique insight into psychoanalytic approaches to transsexuality and the question of assuming a position in gender.

Oren Gozlan, Psy.D. ABPP, is a clinical psychologist and a psychoanalyst in private practice and Professor and Director of clinical training at the Adler Graduate School in Toronto. He is a Diplomate in Psychoanalysis with the American Board of Professional Psychology and is also the Chair of the Gender and Sexuality Committee of the International Forum for Psychoanalytic Education.

Transsexuality and the Art of Transitioning

A Lacanian approach

Oren Gozlan

LONDON AND NEW YORK

First published 2015
by Routledge
27 Church Road, Hove, East Sussex, BN3 2FA

and by Routledge
711 Third Avenue, New York, NY 10017

Routledge is an imprint of the Taylor & Francis Group, an informa business

© 2015 Oren Gozlan

The right of Oren Gozlan to be identified as author of this work has been asserted by him in accordance with sections 77 and 78 of the Copyright, Designs and Patents Act 1988.

All rights reserved. No part of this book may be reprinted or reproduced or utilised in any form or by any electronic, mechanical, or other means, now known or hereafter invented, including photocopying and recording, or in any information storage or retrieval system, without permission in writing from the publishers.

Trademark notice: Product or corporate names may be trademarks or registered trademarks, and are used only for identification and explanation without intent to infringe.

British Library Cataloguing in Publication Data
A catalogue record for this book is available from the British Library

Library of Congress Cataloging-in-Publication Data

Gozlan, Oren.
Transsexuality and the art of transitioning : a lacanian approach / Oren Gozlan.
    pages cm
  1. Transsexualism—Psychological aspects.   2. Transgenderism—Psychological aspects.   3. Gender identity—Psychological aspects.
I. Title.
  HQ77.9.G69 2014
  155.3'3—dc23
  2014009016

ISBN: 978-0-415-85574-7 (hbk)
ISBN: 978-0-415-85575-4 (pbk)
ISBN: 978-1-315-75607-3 (ebk)

Typeset in Times
by Apex CoVantage, LLC

To Agnieszka

Contents

Acknowledgements ix
Introduction xi

1 Transsexuality as a state of mind: questions of learning and indeterminacy 1
Transsexuality of everyday life 3
Embodied apprehension 4
Aesthetic crisis in psychoanalysis 7

2 The aesthetics of transitioning 15
Primal encounters 18
Transsexuality as psychic space 21
Sublimation, perversion and death 23
The art of sublimation 26

3 Narrating transsexuality: transition from memoir to literature 30
Truth or dare: adolescent stories of origin 31
Adolescent belief 37
Reading and writing the body 38
The act of re-writing 40
Phantom writer 43

4 Transsexual surgery: a novel reminder and a navel remainder 47
Identification and the body's excess 48
Transsexuality as sinthome 49
Identification with the act: a clinical fragment 52
Transsexuality, sexual difference and novel beginning 54

5 The "real" time of gender — 58
Cross identification 60
Movement and time in the primary 62
Re-conceptualizing "femininity" 65
Hysteria, femininity and jouissance 66
Matricide and creativity: a question of time 68
Psychoanalysis and the feminine position 69

6 Re-writing the screen — 73
Absence and temporality 74
Ground zero 76
Fantasmatic art of disappearance 78
Between burial and survival 79
Sexual difference as dream 81
The transsexual dream interpretation 83
A return to art 85
The trans-sexuality of thinking and memory 86
The transsexual future of an illusion 88

Conclusion: afterwordness — 90
Scintillation between two deaths 95

References — 97
Index — 101

Acknowledgements

I could not have written *Transsexuality and the Art of Transitioning* without the help of several individuals. I am greatly indebted to Distinguished Professor Dr. Deborah Britzman, for her support and sustained interest in my project. Few contemporary thinkers have done more to elaborate on the strong connection between sexuality and education and broaden the concept of education to include its afterwordness. Britzman's way of treating education as an emotional situation inspired me to consider concepts such as transsexuality as analytic objects. I am deeply thankful for her suggestions and careful reading of several chapters and for presenting me with enigmas when I have reached an impasse in my writing.

I am enormously indebted to Dr. Paola Bohorquez for her gentle, careful and thoughtful editing, comments and stimulating conversations, which helped in clarifying my ideas. I would like to thank Dr. Clarissa Barton for turning my answers into questions and for her intellectual and emotional nourishment throughout the years. I would like to express deep gratitude to Dr. Joshua Levy for helping me develop a third ear with which to listen to my patients and to myself. The *New Directions: Writing and Clinical Thinking from a Psychoanalytic Perspective* program of the Washington Centre of Psychoanalysis, in which I participated for three years, has also provided a safe space where I could test my ideas and cultivate my writing style. I am indebted to my patients who have allowed me into their lives and challenged my thinking. The cover photograph "Transdifferentiation" by Osheen Harruthoonyan (www.osheen.ca) was used with the direct permission of the artist. I would like to thank Osheen for allowing me to use this evocative image as my book cover.

Most of all, I am indebted to my wife whose love, support, insight and containing ways brought moments of coherence to the chaos and volatility inherent to writing.

The author would like to thank Tamar Peleg of New Library for granting permission to reproduce an excerpt from David Grossman's "Falling out of time".

Introduction

Transsexuality is now a "hot topic", and a great deal of contention revolves around what is represented when transsexuality takes the stage. In the therapeutic clinic, transsexuality is usually considered a medical condition, while in cultural life, transsexuality is part of a larger cultural revolution reorienting the nature of identity, sociality and modes of self-fashioning. There is an academic field called "transsexual studies", gay, lesbian, bi-sexual and transgendered political movements, debates on the origin and identities of transgender desire, and a history of discussion of the emergence of the transgendered subject.

To place transsexuality at the centre of a debate regarding origin and politics is indicative of the fact that transsexuality is not a category that is situated in the margins but a phenomenon that raises important questions about gender, identity and sexual difference. However, studies of transsexuality often reflect a latent wish for stability and certainty manifested in the pinning down of categories of normative sexual development or in the medicalization of transsexuality: both strategies, I argue, function as defenses against uncertainty (Britzman, 2009). It is impossible to imagine a study of the human without reference to gender. It is as if we forget how uncertain gender felt at one time in our personal history and decide instead to treat gender as origin, either in social or in biological terms. But what is displaced in the recourse to the certainty of gender is desire. Gender embodiment provides us with the phantasy of completion, a promise of satisfaction. In contrast, enigmatic, unintelligible objects evoke no promise. Like a confrontation with an ambiguous object of art, the concept of transsexuality confronts us with anxieties over not knowing and with a demand to know. But the "despair" (Britzman, 2009, p. 77) over not knowing also reflects the impossibility of the authenticity knowledge. In the despair of loss and lack there is also a desire for "something more" (Britzman, 2009, p. 77).

This book places questions of representation at the heart of transsexuality and, working with clinical, literary, aesthetic and Lacanian formulations, asks what it might mean to consider transsexuality as enacting an enigma that belongs to gender. The enigma can be articulated in this way: can we formulate transsexuality beyond essentialist and constructivist orientations and instead consider transsexuality as belonging to signifying chains involved in and affected by the formation of the unconscious?

This study is characterized by its use of psychoanalysis, suggesting that a transition is needed within psychoanalytic theory and practice in order to question the ways in which psychoanalysis may approach and be affected by the transsexual subject. The purpose of this book, then, is to explore, with psychoanalysis, the transgender field. The reader will find original papers alongside previously published articles that have been revised for this book. Its unique contribution is to challenge the ways we think about transsexuality, moving from biological formulations to psychoanalytic concepts, while providing readers with a new way of thinking about gender as a complex constellation made from within cultural, psycho-social and linguistic structures.

In this book, gender identity is explored through various registers: as desire for the other and for identity, as an imaginary and symbolic link to the other, as a thinking apparatus, as a representation of a phantasy object and as an attempt at representation and an enactment of sexual difference. While this book focuses on the transsexual subject, it examines the ways in which transsexuality can help us expand our understanding and transform our conceptualization of gender and sexual difference within different disciplines. Rather than treating transsexuality as a known subject or attempting to apply preconceived notions of gender to the subject of transsexuality, I turn to art and literature to avoid preconceived ideas that might stabilize its meaning. Like enigmatic objects of art, transsexuality awakens us to what cannot be perceived: the non-gendered aspect of the self, the vulnerability of not knowing, the unknown object of desire that may retrospectively be represented as male or female. This brush with impossibility that produces attempts to symbolize will be explored here as a generative *trans*sexuality – sexuality that does not know its object and is in excess of identity. It is this incompleteness, this insistent lack, which keeps the subject questioning and desiring, what permits her to navigate the unsettling experience of *for*giving, accepting lack, and constructing meaning and sense.

Rather than pinning down transsexuality as a medical or a social category, this study opens up the concept of transsexuality by treating it as an "act of passage", which, like writing, animates the process of representation and meaning making. It is understood, then, as a struggle to symbolize and as a resistance to symbolization. Similarly, the transsexual body presents both an insistence on medicalization and a challenge to it. As the transsexual subject relies on the medical alteration of her body, she must challenge medicalization to give meaning to her experience. Thus, the transsexual subject problematizes our myths of origin. On the one hand, the transsexual is treated as an imposter (Chiland, 2005), pretending to be an original or a new breed, a mutation that diverges from the original male/female. On the other hand, transsexuality rattles the very idea of an origin by opening the question of desire and its effervescent nature. We are reminded of infancy, where gender has no meaning. It is only in latency that the child wonders: "Am I a boy or a girl? Where did I come from? What am I going to be?"

Transsexuality invites us to consider gender as a problem of thinking and of resistance to stability and time, through its simultaneous resistance to and insistence on fixed, totalizing categories. This study addresses practitioners of psychoanalysis and the general reader with the insistence that the inevitable conflict between identity and unconscious is not one that can be settled, thus making those questions that are opened up by transsexuality ("Am I a boy or a girl?" "How does my desire shape my sense of self?") a universal dilemma for the subject. If the potential to "be otherwise" can only arise from the ruins of identity, reason and cultural life (Britzman, 2009, p. 78), we must attempt to dismantle preconceived notions of "other" sexual identity formations and, through a new conceptualization, consider transsexuality as an apparatus for transformation through the disruption it represents to notions of intelligibility, beauty and truth.

In the following chapters, I take up a number of questions: What is transsexuality? How has the psychoanalytic field handled questions of transsexuality? What are the potentials and shortcomings of psychoanalytic approaches to transsexuality? In engaging key psychoanalytic conceptualizations of phantasy, drive, fetish, transference, unconscious, sublimation and sexual difference, I attempt to think transsexuality as a metaphor for the aporia of gender, as a challenge to fixed and totalized understandings of masculinity and femininity, and importantly, as a device through which to continue to unfold the Copernican exigency that defined Freud's original breakthrough.

This study is informed by a Lacanian perspective that locates transsexuality in the intermediate space between the clinic and culture. In undertaking this study, I am joining current conversations around the question of sexual difference under the insistence that identity never fully expresses sexuality and as such, cannot be replaced by gender. Lacan's return to Freud opens up the question of desire, which was bypassed by Freud, in order to problematize the fiction of identity. In this study, Lacan's elaboration of the relations between sexual difference, fantasy and knowledge allow me to think about transsexuality as a bridge between interiority and object relations and to propose a theorization of gender that can tolerate the inchoate.

Transsexuality allows us to think anew the ways in which we locate ourselves vis-a-vis the symbolic order by assuming a gender position. The difficulty is that transsexual choices often position individuals within medical discourses and apparatuses dominated by concerns over normalization and pathology. In turning to aesthetic and literary representations of sexuality and transsexuality, this study hopes to circumvent the simplifications inherent in this model and to critique the normalizing trend that informs much psychoanalytic literature on the subject. While we tend to think of gender as an issue of identity and social recognition, art allows us to rethink sexual identity as an enigma, that is, as an experience traversed by phantasy and affect, conflict and beauty. In turning to art, we may be able to neutralize the history of medicalization of sexuality and to see transsexuality through a new lens: the aesthetics of the emotional world.

In the first chapter I focus on three scenes: The psychoanalytic field, aesthetics and the clinic. I offer a way to think about why transsexuality is treated as a symptom when, in fact, it can be an opportunity to rethink the double bind between nature and culture, a dilemma that often plagues psychoanalytic theories of gender. I develop the thesis that this double bind is reflective of the way in which psychoanalytic theory is inscribed by its own trauma and symptomatically enacts the disavowal of its own difference. I map out some of the ways in which psychoanalysis has missed the point about transsexuality, either by considering it as pathology or by treating it as a known category. I offer a way to link the anxiety that is repeated in psychoanalytic writings about transsexuality with the apparatus psychoanalysis offers to understand transsexuality as a signifier. Here, transsexuality emerges as a metaphor for enigmas of desire and thought, which situate gender as an existential dilemma.

Insofar as it disrupts the fantasy of phallic monism, transsexuality cannot be simply dismissed as pathology while leaving intact a truly psychoanalytic theory of sexual difference. The second chapter focuses more closely on three concepts: transitionality, aesthetic conflict and the question of psychic difference. Through the works of contemporary artists Anish Kapoor and Louise Borgeois, I pose a link between transsexuality as a concept and the experience of handling ambiguity within the self. Focusing on art objects will move us away from transsexuality as a known entity, as a category often applied to a defined and marginalized group and, instead, helps us consider it as an enigmatic experience. I use transsexuality as the lens through which the psychoanalytic theory of sexual difference can be re-examined and offer a reading of the concept of perversion that is closer to Freud's formulation of the polymorphousness of the drive as related to the transitional experience of psychic transformation.

The analytic endeavour creates the possibility of opening imaginary spaces where language addresses the enigma of the body through the act of restructuring and rewriting one's relation to identity itself. Two examples, one literary (*Middlesex*) and one historical (Herculine Barbin), provide us with narratives about other-gendered bodies. I approach these narratives as attempts at psychic transitioning, which often repeat symptomatic answers to the enigmatic nature of sexuality.

The link between repetition and psychic transformation that I begin to elaborate in the first two chapters will continue to be explored in the third chapter through an understanding of gender as the arena on which conflicts around psychic difference are enacted. While in the previous chapters I have used transsexuality as a signifier for the inherent tension between difference and repetition – based on Freud's elaboration of the link between repetition compulsion and the death drive – this chapter illuminates how gender too can be understood as a conflictual articulation of the tension between sexuality and the need for intelligibility. Furthermore, and relying on Freud's concept of the death drive in its relation to sublimation, I consider the analyst's own capacity to sustain the enigma of sexuality as an essential aspect of the analytic experience of transformation, where the patient rewrites history as pathos and is consequently able to enjoy experience as fragmentary and transient.

In Chapter 4 I consider questions of gender integration in transsexuality. While historically the medical/clinical establishment has treated the transsexual's desire for surgery as a hysterical demand, I rely on the Lacanian contributions of Gherovici (2010) and Verhaeghe (2009) to develop the view that transsexual surgery may be understood as a means to traverse the phantasy and claim one's desire. Through the presentation of clinical material, the chapter engages the questions of whether the concept of hysteria is useful when thinking about gender, identity formation and sexual difference, and whether the demand for surgery can be other than a demand for certitude.

Through a clinical case involving a self identified transsexual who is oscillating between genders, Chapter 5 explores another way in which we can think of gender as a marker of difference and its disavowal. The case allows us to think of how gender's failure to fully contain or inscribe sexuality allows it to be used defensively to obliterate difference. The case also highlights the necessity of unchaining conceptions of gender. Moving away from a priori biological and cultural meanings, Chapter 5 introduces gender to the timeless process of analysis where signifiers do not possess univocal meanings but constitute, instead, unstable representations of unique associative paths and clusters of meaning.

The question of what would it mean to shatter the concept of gender and to live with the realization of its fragility will be explored in Chapter 6. This chapter returns to the role of aesthetic conflict in psychic transformation and resituates enigma as structured by and as structuring of the unconscious. I draw on Jonathan Lear's book *Radical hope* (2006) to consider the inherent relationship between interpretation, imagination and intelligibility in the context of devastating psychic transformation. In facing the end to the buffalo-hunting way of life, Plenty Coups' reflexive stance enabled his tribe to work through and come to terms with a catastrophic loss of intelligibility. In this chapter, Plenty Coups' interpretation is considered as a metaphor for the analytic process by exploring the difference between repetition and narration as it applies to the concept of gender.

Earlier versions of two chapters have been published elsewhere. An original version of Chapter 4 was published in the International Forum of Psychoanalysis, Volume 20, 2011 and reproduced by permission of Routledge/Taylor and Francis Group, LLC. An earlier version of Chapter 5 was published in the European Journal of Psychoanalysis, Number 30, 2010 (I) and reproduced with permission of IPOC Italian Paths of Culture.

The case examples used in this book are an amalgamation of a number of patients and do not refer to an actual patient.

Chapter 1

Transsexuality as a state of mind

Questions of learning and indeterminacy

> *His death makes me into an empty soughing of a father and mother, extract a breast within me . . . thus, with a transparent scalpel, his death carves new knowledge in me: loss is forever feminine.*
> David Grossman, From *Falling out of time*

In contemporary cultural life, the visibility of transsexuality is part of a larger cultural revolution reorienting the nature of identity, sociality and modes of self-fashioning. The therapeutic clinic, however, lags behind: transsexuality is still considered a pathological condition. Historically, psychoanalysis has approached the experience of transsexuality through questions of "gender certainty" and "sexual difference", often invoked as separating the boundaries between normalcy and pathology. Contemporary theories of gender (e.g. Benjamin, 1998; Dimen, 2003; Harris, 2005) attempt to de-pathologize transsexuality, although these theories often treat gender categories as sociological descriptors. Even when masculinity and femininity are approached as psychic positions (e.g. Gherovici, 2010), discussions are often limited to "the transsexual individual". Missing is a conceptualization of transsexuality as a psychical position and discussions on how its subject formation affects the imaginary of psychoanalysis. In this book, I attempt to broaden our conception of transsexuality, shifting the focus from the "transsexual patient" to the analyst's thought processes. I do so by considering questions of desire, sexuality and sexual difference.

The main claim throughout this book involves what I consider to be the phenomenological dimension of transsexuality, understood both as a transformation at the level of the flesh and as a term that captures the universality of sexuality, which is always transformative and in transit. I argue for the need for an aesthetic shift in psychoanalytic discourse, one capable of understanding sexuality as always already in transition (Gozlan, 2011). Mainly, I hope to show that, like the aesthetic object, sexual difference does not embody intent but, rather, constitutes the unrepresentable tension that the gender binary both enacts and veils. In taking an aesthetic approach to the question of transsexuality, I intend to signify the difficult encounter with the fragility of knowledge and certainty, as conditions for creativity and thought that open the subject to his or her own difference.

In my psychoanalytic practice, I often encounter patients who express certainty about who they are but whose bodies do not match their perception of being situated in gender as male or female. For many such patients, the body becomes a battle ground where the urgency to settle into one gender becomes heightened by the felt impossibility of reaching such certainty. The body sabotages the desire to be a man or a woman and is often hated for not being "masculine or feminine enough". Such patients often perceive this incongruity between their body and the language of male/female as intolerable and they often yearn for complete harmony between body and psychic identification. Many transgender and transsexual individuals I see in my practice are preoccupied with their discomfort over the perceived indeterminacy of their bodies, anxious about not being recognized in their desired gender or, even worse, threatened by being perceived as strange, abject, repulsive bodies.

The narratives accompanying this frustration are often laced with fantasies of an idealized embodiment, which often prevents these patients from experiencing satisfaction with and relative settlement in their given bodies. Statements such as "I am not a 'real' man/woman" are accompanied with mute fights with the body through skin picking, cutting, anorexia and other forms of self-injury. Narratives of exciting pre-adolescent years are quite common among these patients. They share memories of the thrill of wearing clothes of "the other sex", tinged with a sense of the forbidden or a seeming carelessness about one's gender and objects of desire. Pre-pubescent years are often described as a time of exploration and excitement about the open possibilities. For some, however, memories of adolescence contain a sense of despair, a self-punishing sense of transgression and chaos, often articulated in repetitive, nostalgic and melancholic narratives. The wish to be a "real" man/woman paired with the sense of not being "good enough" in either imagined embodiment speak to the fantasy of having a body that is "outside" or "beyond" sex, one that transgresses the law of sexual difference. The fantasy of the wholeness of sex and hence of ultimate satisfaction that often lurks behind this desire becomes an obstacle to enjoyment as the psychic experience of one's sexual embodiment does not coincide with a body that always fails.

It is tempting to stay with clinic and wonder about the meaning of the transsexual plea. However, in limiting our examination to the clinic and to the experience of "the transsexual patient" we are at risk of failing to attend to larger questions of sexual identity and desire and their role in subject formation. We cease, for example, to consider the role of sexuality in psychic organization, to pose the question of how sexuality disrupts or enlivens the "ground of being" (Parker, 2011, p.16). The moment we consider questions of desire and embodiment, wholeness and impossibility, satisfaction and transgression, as embedded in the experience of transsexuality, we are engaging with the imaginary, symbolic and real registers of sexuality as human experience. These Lacanian categories are helpful for conceptualizing transsexuality beyond the pathologization characteristic of medical and psychiatric discourses.

My orientation follows the Lacanian view that analytic listening is placed on absence, silences, omissions, gaps in meaning and the question of desire. The analyst may not fill the absence with meaning, and while the analytic encounter is not a corrective experience, it serves as a fragile symbolic link between the self and other. It is meant to awake an enigma and with it, the potential for desire and less debilitating self-definitions. This focus on absence understands language as fragmenting, castrating, but also as providing a signifying difference that opens up previously closed circuits of meaning. Once transsexuality is imagined as psychical experience, we may enter into questions of truth, beauty and knowledge and the tensions between them. Meltzer approaches these questions in relation to the apprehension of the mother's body.

Transsexuality of everyday life

Meltzer poses the beauty of the mother's body as the first enigmatic object for the infant and names this encounter an "aesthetic conflict" (2008). Here is where the conflict begins: something cannot be seen and it is with the invisible that the baby is preoccupied. The baby's interest in what is inside the (m)other's body leaves a trace, a problem of origin and a demand to understand. Meltzer posits the encounter of the baby with the infinite enigma of the maternal body as both satisfying and violent because satisfaction is also experienced as violating the limits of the infant's body. Hence, our first position in relation to beauty is ambivalent in the sense that such beauty stands before the child, it is not a creation of the child. The baby feels he is the creator of the breast, yet experiences the breast as otherness through its unavailability. In this sense, the beauty and enigmatic character of the mother's otherness disrupts the infant's primary narcissism and inaugurates a conflict between sensual apprehension and creative imagination, "between the inside and the outside, between essence and appearance, and between presence and absence" (Britzman, forthcoming).

The notion of aesthetic conflict allows us to conceptualize the subject's gradual capacity to register otherness, before and beyond words. The enigmatic presence of the other arouses curiosity and allows questions and doubt, thus calling forth a search for meaning that constitutes the grounds for connection and intimacy. But doubt also brings forth anxiety and pain that often stirs a violent wish to see the other's insides. It is in between this search for knowledge and truth, on the one hand, and fantasies of intrusive projective identification, on the other, that the subject walks the narrow path of imagination.

Meltzer posits a link between aesthetic conflict, on the one hand, and dynamics of thought and relationality on the other, where the experience of satisfaction is often accompanied by a sense of violation through the registration of difference. Such violation of boundaries experienced through the registration of care – which Meltzer describes as a "mindless" operation (p. 68) – entails the employment of received symbols functioning "as signs" (p. 68), as well as exchanges of sight, touch, smell, pain and pleasure between mother and infant. The apprehension of beauty occurs in and through these exchanges in the form of compromise formations that involve pleasure, captivation, fear, suspense and weariness, and which inaugurate the capacity for sublimation. There is a violence implicit in such sensorial and affective apprehension of the object, for the registration of its otherness prompts its disavowal as a way to reduce the tension of aesthetic conflict. The aesthetic conflict, in other words, captures the way in which the infant, in her need for emotional contact, attempts to degrade the object as known and certain. The encounter with the enigma of the primal (desiring) parental body triggers a turbulent desire to know, that is, to break the barrier between inside and outside. Fragmenting the other into partial objects where the parental body is treated as an "inanimate machine" or as "matter like faeces" (Meltzer, 2008, p. 73) is a common mechanism that attempts to transform the other from unidentifiable into recognizable and hence to degrade the object by denying its foreboding otherness. Since the impacting other is also an internalized object, the degradation of the object through splitting is also an attack on self-difference and, therefore, on thinking.

As a gradually developing capacity to create psychic space, a transitional area of both impasse and connection, thinking involves the possibility of holding things in one's mind, where emotional experience is stored as memory rather than acted out. Heidegger conceives of thinking as a "holding steady" (Heidegger, 1966, p. 62) thus reconceptualizing what is often understood as a deliberate seeking into a restrained "waiting". This presupposes both the development of psychic space and the temporalization of experience. It is a process, in short, that involves the "becoming-time of space and the becoming-space of time" (Derrida, 1982, p. 8). The creation of internal transitional space is linked with the process of apprehension of beauty. What is apprehended is the affect evoked through the experience of aesthetic conflict that becomes tolerable through its links with an internalized object of care. In this sense, the apprehension of beauty is a necessary condition for the creation of internal transitional space, where the tension between the registration of the parental other as an object of care that, nevertheless, remains enigmatic, can be sustained. To tolerate the experience of transitionality means, therefore, to sustain the inner tension of the differentiating encounter with the other through one's curiosity and the ability to embody the psychic conflict.

Embodied apprehension

Thinking about the transsexual body as a place of emotional meaning, and hence as a psychic position, opens the question of how gender elicits an aesthetic conflict. If gender functions as a veil for the constitutive instability of the subject split by her unconscious, it can be argued that every gender disposition carries a kernel of helplessness, anxiety and guilt, and therefore it is vulnerable to dissociation, splitting and idealization. Meltzer's conceptualization of the apprehension of beauty captures the paradox of grasping and simultaneously being unsettled by the other's enigmatic body. While Winnicott understands the aesthetic encounter mainly as an experience of continuity and holding (Winnicott, 1971), Meltzer's notion of aesthetic conflict signals both the containing and disruptive qualities of the experience of apprehension of beauty. This paradox that is experienced in the encounter between the infant and the mother is also experienced, I argue, with objects of art and the transsexual body, thus producing an ambivalent affective scenario. In other words, the encounter with the transsexual body and with the object of art constitutes an opportunity to apprehend and be apprehended by the difference registered through embodied experiences of transitionality. Both the insufficiency of gender categorizations in signifying the ambiguous body and the inadequacy of our sensibility and imagination in making sense of the enigmatic object of art hold the potential and risks that Meltzer identifies at the core of the aesthetic conflict.

The desire to apprehend the beautiful and enigmatic object carries within it the tension aroused by an uncertainty that is also the foundation of desire. In thinking through the enigma elicited by the ambiguously gendered body, gender reveals itself as a paradoxical concept, simultaneously a placeholder that sustains the tension of sexual difference, and a concretization of desire's polymorphous nature. Accordingly, to think of gender as an aesthetic category, as a space for the apprehension of beauty, means to consider its role in the registration and denial of difference. As a response to the enigma of desire, the concept of gender involves both the degradation of the ambiguous object through splitting and concretization and, at the same time, it functions as a signifier that holds beauty, truth and knowledge in tension. The interpellation of gender is both a conscious and an unconscious hailing of the child that positions her in a symbolic system of sexual difference from birth, or even before. It is sustained by the unconscious maternal environment, which includes not only the mother's unconscious desire but the totality of her history, an environment that is continually reinforced by a social discourse that is all encompassing and whose boundaries – its own self-difference – are impossible to identify. Gender is both culture's response to unconscious difference and, at the same time, an attempt to render sexual difference legible by eradicating difference itself. In other words, insofar as the dichotomy masculine/feminine ultimately holds the promises of the wholeness of sexual identity and the complementarity between the genders, it ultimately fails both to inscribe and eradicate the enigma of sexual difference; sexuality remains, therefore, an ever-proliferating question, which no gender division can stabilize. As Žižek argues, rather than closing up the question of sexuation, the real of sexual difference reveals the arbitrary and insufficient character of every symbolic articulation of the gender divide: "Every translation of sexual difference into a set of symbolic opposition(s) is doomed to fail, and it is this very 'impossibility' that opens up the terrain of the hegemonic struggle for what 'sexual difference' will mean" (Žižek, 2002, p. 61).

As a form of knowing, gender functions as a process of identification with the unconscious naming of the other that defends the subject against the polymorphous perversity of desire: always accidental and in flux. Yet, gender is also repetition of that which it attempts to eradicate insofar as it also holds a trace of the polymorphous perversity of the drive, a promise of a return to a state of satisfaction through a phantasy of wholeness in self-coincidence and unity through the complementarity of gender.

The notion of gender as a conflictual attempt to both signify and eradicate difference is echoed in Winnicott's understanding of femininity and masculinity as internal positions in relation to the unknown of the mother's body (Winnicott, 1971). For Winnicott, these positions define subjectivity and are independent of genital sex. They represent, respectively, "being" and "doing", passivity and activity, as responses to the enigmatic encounter with the otherness of the maternal body. "Being" implies tolerance toward one's passive stance in relation to the unknown, to difference, but it is also a "maiming" because it signifies a dependency on an intractable exteriority that survives the baby's ruthless attacks (Winnicott, 1971). "Being" is contrasted with "doing", which refers to the quest for satisfaction, the need to act as if one could know, possess and control time and gender; a position saturated with certitude and, as such, omnipotent. Certitude, however, can never be sure of its own certainty; it constitutes an anxious response to the ambiguity and instability of the psychic object, a necrotizing response to transitionality and a symbolic equation that attempts to collapse the space between self and object. In contrast, Winnicott argues, recognition of the transitionality inherent in object-relating is a condition for symbolization.

Lacan also treats femininity and masculinity as psychic positions in relation to the unknown of desire (Lacan, 1999). Understood as positions in relation to one's self-otherness, assuming a gender signifies an acceptance of an answer regarding one's place in the symbolic order. While one can identify as male or female and hold on to notions of femininity or masculinity as coherent categories, this gender certainty represents an attempt to obliterate the difference within the self and to domesticate the "real of sex", that is, the non-metabolizable kernel that resists meaning or symbolization. In this model, gender certainty become aligned with phallic mastery and power while the remainder, which cannot be symbolized, is associated with the feminine, which stands in helpless relation to the Real. Femininity here does not represent a gender, but a psychic position that goes beyond the phallic structure of "castrated" "non-castrated", and as such, it does not constitute an "answer" to the real of sex. Rather, it is linked with the traumatic Real (Verhaeghe, 2001, p. 38) that cannot be signified, and in this way, enigmatic and transitional.

Lacan's and Winnicott's conceptions of femininity and masculinity are helpful in theorizing sexual difference as psychic positions that exceed symbolic articulation, that is, as always incomplete identifications which fail to contain the real of sexual difference. In Winnicott's terms, a transitional space or object does not mark a point where the harmonious integration of drive and culture is achieved. On the contrary, it is a space where the impossibility of such integration is tolerated through compromise formations, which allow for creative resignifications. In this sense, transitional spaces and objects allow for the experience of "living in suspense", as the capacity to accept reality as an always-shifting compromise formation, never absolute, always in question.

Artistic expression constitutes for Winnicott one of the paradigmatic forms of the experience of the "in-between", a transitional area between internal and external reality (Winnicott, 1971). The creative object holds meaning and constitutes a symbol of what cannot be fully represented. It is a placeholder that sustains the ambiguous relation between desire and knowledge, yet translates this instability into tolerable tension through its plasticity, a malleable link between the literal and the metaphoric. The object of art is never in charge of itself (Britzman, 2009), it can never completely express or satisfy the subject's desire and, in its effervescence, opens the subject to his or her own lack. The uncanny inexhaustibility that characterizes the in-between experience of the artistic encounter resonates with questions of embodiment and the way in which the body's estrangement always exceeds the literalness of our symbolic articulations of gender. I, therefore, find in art a metaphor for narrating a set of preoccupations that concern the dispersal of desire and its polymorphous nature, along with an embodied response to this dispersal. In examining Anish Kapoor's art, in particular his installation "Memory", and a sample of Louise Bourgeois' work, I want to understand how the creation of such intermediate space produces a form of aesthetic crisis for the viewer.

Like the aesthetic crisis produced by Kapoor's spectacular installations, the encounter with transsexuality can interrupt our imaginary certainty of gender. I propose, then, that transsexuality can be thought of as a placeholder for the incommensurability between gender and sexual difference. To the extent that the transsexual's peculiar response to the symbolic demand to situate ourselves in gender makes apparent this irresolvable tension, I argue that the encounter with the transsexual body may bring forth an aesthetic crisis that destabilizes our gender certitude, thus inviting us to confront anew the enigma of our sexual identifications.

Aesthetic crisis in psychoanalysis

By and large, the transsexual subject is thought of as a problematic figure whose insistence on becoming a "real" man or woman is seen as an inability to accept the limits of the sexed body. As the theory goes, the transsexual treats his/her body as a fetish in her/his struggle with the presence or absence of the penis and, therefore, the desire for surgery is seen as a means to become a complete, whole subject. Sex reassignment surgery is interpreted as evidence for such conceptualization, and is construed as an omnipotent attempt to enact a phantasy of re-birth or reach an ideal construction of self through the transformation of one's biological sex.

What is problematic about such conceptualizations, however, is the disavowal of the fundamental Freudian insight that fetishism is inherent to the imaginary construction of gender. From this perspective one could argue that any claim to identity involves a "mystification" of the phallus, a certain degree of concretization and certitude.

In examining what he terms "infantile sexual theories" Freud (1905) universalizes the role of fetishism as the mechanism through which the psyche simultaneously registers and disavows the maternal phallus. The simultaneous denial and recognition of the absence of the maternal phallus (castration) can only be maintained through the fetishistic eroticization of an object that comes to represent absence. Because the fetish functions as a veil that both signals and hides the absence of the maternal phallus, it serves as a defense against a traumatic perception (the absence of the penis) and as a transitional object with the potential to be used as an enigmatic object that facilitates transition (temporalization) through the work of the imagination. To the extent that the fetish can function as a transitional object, it can potentially unite materiality with phantasy.

And yet, as Bass observes (2000), Freud's theory of sexual difference reiterates the same fetishistic thinking that his theory is meant to explain insofar as it treats castration as fact rather than as fantasy, thus reinforcing the phallic monism that characterizes his theories' infantile sexuality. In other words, in arguing that the fetishist disavows the "fact of castration", Freud forgets that castration is as much a fantasy as is the maternal phallus and, therefore, that to embrace the reality of sexual difference what needs to be overcome is the fetishistic phantasy of phallic monism (non-castrated/castrated). From this perspective one could argue that transsexuality cannot be defined by fetishization, as the mystification of the phallus (treating castration as certainty) is universal.

This normative framework runs counter to psychoanalysis' fundamental insight into the essentially unstable and fragile nature of sexual identification and the polymorphous character of the drive, where the absence or presence of the penis is but a veil for a "deeper" absence. Indeed, in proposing that the relation between the drive and its object is arbitrary, Freud establishes the accidental nature of gender identifications and the unpredictability of desire. The arbitrariness of the drive's choice of object gives sexuality its perverse character. Insofar as it disrupts the fantasy of phallic monism, transsexuality cannot be simply dismissed as pathology while leaving intact the psychoanalytic theory of sexual difference. In line with Laplanche's idea that the development of psychoanalytic theory "reproduces the fate of sexuality and the unconscious in the human being" (Laplanche, 1999 p. 3), I suggest that we consider transsexuality as that which reveals psychoanalysis' ambiguous investment in normative sexuality while simultaneously problematizing its disavowal of the heterogeneity of the drive. Furthermore, I suggest that psychoanalysis is haunted by its own unconscious trauma, that is, by its resistance to the fundamental insight that sexuality is thoroughly traversed by the unconscious, a resistance that leads to a fetishistic understanding of transsexuality.

Psychoanalytic theories of transsexuality are themselves caught in the aporetic encounter between nature and culture, normative sexuality and polymorphous perversion, but are seldom able to hold in tension the traumatic quality of that which cannot be known or the implications of the irreconcilability of these terms. I would like to formulate transsexuality as a psychic position and as a metaphor for the transitional experience of the transformation of the psyche. I will consider transsexuality through an aesthetic approach to the question of sexual difference under the assumption that transsexuality may open rigid, naturalized and concretized understandings of gender. I am going to think about transsexuality as an experience that thwarts the ideal of subjectivity.

An edited collection of essays published in 2009 titled *Transvestism, transsexualism in the psychoanalytic dimension,* compiled by Giovanna Ambrosio, provides a paradigmatic example of the way in which sexual difference is approached in normative psychoanalytic discourse. While the editor acknowledges that to reflect on the issue of transsexuality requires coming to terms with "the difficult interweaving" of "medical, legal, and social complexities" (Ambrosio, 2009, p. xvi), and furthermore admonishes on the need to "guard ourselves against every kind of ideological conformism" (Ambrosio, 2009, p. xvi), the collection reflects the institutional position of the International Psychoanalytic Association regarding transsexuality and other "shaded areas of sexuality" (Ambrosio, 2009, p. xiii), which are, from the very start, classified within the "disorders of sexual identity or gender identity" (Ambrosio, 2009, p. xvi):

> We all seem to agree on the pathological and diversified nature of transvestism and transsexualism, with the exception of passing or mixed forms of the same ... While transvestism corresponds to a more developed stage of the processes of individuation-separation, the Winnicottian transitional area, transsexualism binds the thought process to the concreteness of the body, thus signaling the absence of symbolic thought.
>
> (Ambrosio, 2009, p. xix)

While the authors are also said to agree that analytic neutrality is an essential tool that "allows us to unveil, enter in contact with and give voice to all parts of our patient" (Ambrosio, 2009, p. xxi), the way in which *the transsexual* patient is assumed to be a *known object,* one preemptively categorized as deviant, defines those "shaded areas of sexuality" as always and already deciphered within an all-encompassing and closed system of thought in which sexual difference is concretized as biological sex. This is particularly puzzling in light of recent discussions, which have addressed what is called "transsexual certainty" – the transsexual's conviction of the discontinuity between her/his gender and sex. Wolff-Bernstein, for instance, suggests that this certainty – "the knowing what (*they*) are" (2011, p. 5) – places the transsexual solution closer to the psychotic structure insofar as it represents "a delusional system that substitutes for the foreclosed name of the father" (Wolff-Bernstein, 2011 p. 5). Following a fetishistic treatment of gender, Wolff-Bernstein is unaware of the contradiction inherent in treating the transsexual identification as delusional because it denies what is understood to be "the reality of castration", whose acceptance is equated here with accepting the law of "the name of the father". The transsexual's desire to allegedly "correct an error in the real of the body" (Gherovici, 2010, p. 195), that is, his/her concretizing experience of gender, is placed here in opposition to the non-transsexual's assumed capacity to treat gender "symbolically". Statements such as these not only manage to obscure the "gender certainty" enjoyed by most heteronormative individuals whose gender identity's experience happens to coincide with their biological sex, but also, and perhaps more troublesome, psychoanalysis' own complicity with a heteronormative ideology, which, paradoxically, is incompatible with the analytic theorization of the process of sexuation. The problematic assumption that heterosexuality, de facto, implies symbolic apprehension of gender reflects a denial of the way in which heteronormative subjectivity and desire is treated as given, as if heteronormative sexuality and the process through which it comes into being did not require thinking.

Psychoanalytic discourse, however, insists upon the tolerance of confusion, anxiety and ambivalence as a necessary condition for creating a psychic space; it invites us to consider the enigmatic nature of sexuality, and through the transference, to open the psyche to its own difference. As a theory of otherness, psychoanalysis needs to examine critically its own investment and complicity in normative discourses of gender while simultaneously allowing itself to be affected and displaced by what non-normative forms of sexed embodiment can teach us about subjectivity and desire. In the same manner, and as a condition for an ethical analytical process, the analyst needs to be alert to her identification with the position of the "subject supposed to know", and therefore, be capable of questioning her own certainty and infallibility regarding her understanding of the transsexual patient who comes, as all patients do, with doubts about the veracity of their self-narrative, their personal truth. Lacan warns against certitude and the temptation to approach concepts in a deadening way by insisting on treating concepts analytically, that is, by dislodging them from saturated, opaque meanings while reflecting on their subjective foundation (Lacan, 1977). Through this warning, Lacan alerts us against a necrotizing tendency in theory itself as a defense against thinking. To the extent that the psychoanalytic theory of sexuation is itself affected by the trauma of sexuality and transferentially implicated in its irreducible otherness, it runs the risk of hardening defensively against the inexhaustible insistence of sexuality. In theorizing transsexuality as a psychic position, I attempt to illuminate some of the ways in which psychoanalytic theory is affected and effected by the trauma of sexual difference and how it repeats, through projective identification, its own anxieties over unintelligibility, fragmentation and transgression.

We are left with questions about the tendency to pathologize transsexuality. Why, for instance, are these theories blind to the heteronormative privilege embedded in the conflation between gender and sex? Do these conceptual approaches consider the contingent association of sex with gender as a psychic achievement against which all other forms of sexual identification are to be measured? How does the tendency to pathologize transsexuality foreclose questions regarding the imbrication of nature and culture? Conversely, would taking seriously the problem of transsexuality open up opportunities to re-examine psychoanalytic theories of gender identity formation? I would like to put forward the idea that the tendency to pathologize transsexuality is indicative of a tremendous anxiety around the phantasy of the transsexual as wreaking havoc on "nature", a presumed natural order that is often and erroneously conflated with the law of the symbolic order.

In order to examine this idea, I would like first to take a detour through various approximations to the questions of sexed identity.

In *The Accident of Gender* (2008), I proposed to think the concept of gender as a traumatic formation through which to understand a pervasive tendency in psychoanalytic thinking to collapse sexual difference with a concrete choice: that of "having" or "being" the phallus. I have conceptualized this dualism as a defensive attempt to stabilize the otherness represented by the unconscious, where sexual difference is articulated through castration as an anchoring point of identity and containment strategy for the anxiety of (self) difference. As I have argued, this binary model, which relies on the acceptance of "the reality of castration" – the presence or absence of the penis – as the grounds of sexual difference, can only reduce transsexuality to a pathological formation predicated on the refusal to accept the real of the sexed body.

In contrast to the normative psychoanalytic position, constructivist theorists of gender such as Butler (1990), Benjamin (1998) and Harris (2005) focus on the sociocultural and discursive dimensions of gender relations and identities and, as a consequence, offer a more open view of transsexuality and other non-normative forms of sexual embodiment. Butler, for instance, privileges the question of how the seeming unity of biological sex, gendered identification and heterosexual desire is constructed as natural through discourses and social practices. In the work of Harris, gender is conceptualized as a "soft assembly" (2005) that gives expression to multiple identities across a spectrum of practices and desires. In this direction, she suggests that it might be helpful "to maintain a contradictory model of gender in which it is a serious, fully lived, conscious experience of self, often 'core' to one's being, and at the same time, it can dissolve or transmute under our very gaze" (Harris, 2002, p. 113). Finally, and informed by object-relations theory, Benjamin focuses on the historically constituted and intersubjective nature of gender relations in an attempt to critique the dichotomization of sexed identity into masculine/active/dominant and feminine/passive/submissive. While these contributions have undoubtedly illuminated the sociocultural, historical and political dimensions of processes of gender formation, their efforts to de-essentialize and denaturalize gender have occluded the extra-discursive dimension of sexed identity: the real of the body. As Dean argues (2000), approaching gender solely in identity terms, that is, as consciously formulated and discursively articulated in its entirety, constitutes a form of "philosophical voluntarism" (Dean, 2000, p. 78) predicated on the idea that reality can be changed at will and, correspondingly that "gender is fully manipulable" (Dean, 2000, p. 74). In agreement with Dean, I would argue that it is through an account of sexuality that holds in tension the conflictual imbrication between the symbolic, the imaginary and the real that the deadlock between essentialism and constructivism can be sublated. Furthermore, to consider the function of the real, the extra-discursive dimension of sexuality, is particularly important in thinking transsexuality insofar as the transsexual claim seems to be about securing gender certainty as sex in the body.

While it is clear that sexuality cannot be thought of outside of its sociocultural articulations – and in this sense it is helpful to remember that "there are many symbolic orders, many interwoven networks of signifiers through which we move" (Dean, 2000, p. 18) – it is also crucial to assert that sexuality insistently thwarts such sociocultural articulations of identity and desire. What the constructivist theories of gender fail to examine is the way in which sexuality is better apprehended through the systematic failure of such interpellations, through their necessary incomplete and fragmentary nature. Conversely, the symbolic order itself emerges partly as a response to the enigmatic and traumatic character of sexuality, which is always in excess of the signifier. As both Freud and Lacan argue, sexuality is inherently paradoxical and decentring: always heterogeneous to the ego and temporally out of joint. Discourse itself is a response to the otherness of the unconscious, to its radical heterogeneity from secondary processes of signification governed by the conscious registration of spatio-temporal difference. Moreover, the fact that there is no signifier for sexual difference in the unconscious, as Lacan argues, can only intensify the incommensurability between the symbolic, imaginary and real dimensions of sexual identity. This gives us an entry point to think about transsexuality as a question related to the enigma of sexual difference that is not simply a problem for the transsexual subject.

To take the idea of the unconscious seriously means that we must account for its influence on the construction of cultural discourse. While Butler views social practices, discourses and regulations as shaping sexuality, psychoanalysis approaches culture and sexuality as intertwined and influencing each other. Yet, while sexuality finds expression in a myriad of symbolic and imaginary articulations, it is fundamentally disruptive of such arrangements because it is polymorphously perverse and decentring, hence, enigmatic and anxiety provoking. Tim Dean argues that the fact that there is no signifier for sexual difference in the unconscious means that "sexual difference does not organize or determine sexual desire" (Dean, 2000, p. 87). The implications of this psychoanalytic postulate are far reaching and its potential to destabilize normative gender discourses can hardly be overstated. Indeed, if the real of sexual difference opens rather than closes sexual desire to a myriad of contingent configurations, then we can argue that heteronormative discourse, in its insistence on a univocal relationship between sexual difference, gender identity and desire, represents an attempt to hinder the proliferation of possible sexual arrangements.

Considered psychoanalytically, then, transsexuality ceases to refer to a known phenomenon specific to identifiable subjects and, instead, can be approached as a particular embodiment of sexual difference that captures a universal enigma at the heart of subjectivity. This enigma can be described as a tension already embedded in primal narcissism, which, as Bass argues, constitutes a state of simultaneous registration and repudiation of difference: "the registration of something *other* than oneself which *is* also oneself" (Bass, 2006, p. 19). To make sense of this aporia, it is important to remember that, before the development of the distinction between self and other, the unconscious apprehends difference through the registration of the experience of satisfaction that creates an unconscious memory of tension relief, the very memory that the infant re-cathacts, as a tension reduction mechanism, in the experience of hallucinatory wish fulfilment. Thus, "the transformation of difference into identity through wish fulfilment is the 'origin' of unconscious transformation of an intrinsically open to an apparently closed system" (Bass, 2006, p. 33). This tendency to transform difference into identity is not unique to primary narcissism; on the contrary, it is the dedifferentiating propensity that the psychoanalytic therapy aims to contrast.

One could argue that the myriad of psychic processes through which one comes to assume a particular sexual embodiment occurs through the simultaneous registration and repudiation of self-difference. When gender is assumed as naturally given, or, on the other extreme of the continuum, as "a matter of choice" (Gherovici, 2010), what gets foreclosed is the incommensurability between the symbolic articulation of gender and the real of sexual difference, which is itself the tension rising force of unconscious differentiation.

The demand to articulate fully and without remainder the deadlock of internal difference is elaborated in particular ways through the question of transsexuality. For the transsexual subject, the dilemma may be expressed as the wish to have the cohesive body that the other is assumed to have. In turn, the anxiety that the transsexual body evokes around questions of intelligibility and symbolic legitimacy makes apparent our need to disavow the uncertainty that every gender identification veils. The projection of lack, insufficiency and excess onto the transsexual body reveals that the phantasy of cohesion implicit in the fiction of identity is in itself a container for the anxiety over unconscious undecidability, for, as psychoanalysis reminds us, the accidental match between the sexed body and gender identity is tenuous and fragile at best.

I have suggested that psychoanalytic discourse moves ambivalently between the compulsion to uphold the normative binary gender system and the desire to give voice to the radical heterogeneity of the drive. Given this oscillation, I would like to suggest that through the lens of transsexuality, the psychoanalytic theory of sexual difference can be reexamined in ways that illuminate its unthought investments and anxieties, its defenses against the trauma of difference and its repetition of the deadlock of desire. In other words, I am suggesting that, insofar as analytic discourse constitutes itself in response to the trauma of sexual difference, it inevitably becomes inflected by this trauma. Through a conceptual shift that opens the question of transsexuality to its otherness – as other to its imaginary meaning – psychoanalytic discourse may become destabilized through a reconsideration of transsexuality, which, like femininity and masculinity, demands interpretation rather than normative valuation. A psychoanalytic study that addresses transsexuality must therefore be framed by the insistence that the inevitable conflict between identity and unconscious, time and timelessness, subject and object, is not one that can be settled outside of the interpretative process that defines psychoanalytic thought, which revolves around the question of "how the cut can tie a knot, or inversely, how the link can be interruption itself" (Derrida, 1998, p. 12).

In this way, the explicit question that the transsexual brings to analysis – "Am I a boy or a girl?" – can be properly understood as a dilemma for every subjectivity and gender formation.

Transitioning our thinking about transsexuality from a category of identity to a problem of aesthetics requires us to consider the experience of conceptual breakdown as the grounds for transformation and a new education. Britzman asks us to conceptualize education as an "unsolved problem" (2011, p. 23) that inevitably calls forth defenses but also "permits new learning dispositions" (2011, p. 23). She reminds us that psychoanalysis invites us to resist closure and to consider the inherent impasse between body and language. At its best, psychoanalytic thought is always unfinished, uncertain of itself and open to its own collapse. Can we understand, then, the collapse in psychoanalytic discourse around the topic of transsexuality as a problem of education that also belongs to the trauma of learning gender? I suggest that we can treat transsexuality as an enigmatic signifier, an unconscious representation of a structural deadlock that cannot be reduced to the historical and contingent conditions that define our current hegemonic regime of sexual difference. This approach would require us to empty the construct of transsexuality from its "known" biological, social and medical meanings in order to suspend it as an object of phantasy; that is, as an object through which the void of selfhood and desire materializes itself.

In the next chapter, I turn to an interpretation of a series of visual art objects in order to suggest that to think analytically about transsexuality not only requires consideration of multiple perspectives but also, and perhaps more importantly, a realization that every perspective is always multiple insofar as it holds its own phantasy as well as what exceeds its own field of vision. I want to advance the idea that these enigmatic art objects – not unlike transsexuality – shatter the imaginary container that is gender, of its intelligibility. Thinking of the image of the transsexual body through the enigmatic, pleasurable, erotic and destabilizing effects of such art objects, and thinking of art, conversely, as a metaphor for the unpredictable course of embodiment, moves us closer to the enigmatic nature of desire that does not know its object but finds truth in its beauty. Through its enigmatic indecipherability, art confronts us once again with the murkiness of childhood experience, that is, with its conflation of subject and object, reality and fantasy, perception and imagination. Through this approach that focuses on the imagination, we may also soften our hold on gender certainty. Considered both as a fetishistic response to difference and as a place holder for desire, which, like the aesthetic object, is enjoyed for its transitional qualities, gender can be approached as an imaginative container that both differentiates and defers satisfaction, as a conglomerate of multiple, partial and conflictual identifications that do not necessarily harmonize in the mirage of *identity*.

Chapter 2

The aesthetics of transitioning

To open the concept of gender to its oscillations, this chapter turns to the works of the sculptor Anish Kapoor, in particular to his sculpture titled "Memory",[1] and to the work of French artist Louise Bourgeois. I find Kapoor's and Bourgeois' work captivating in their capacity to invoke terror and awe, fullness and emptiness, tenderness and violence. Their work seems to capture the threshold between body and psyche, the "extimate" (Lacan, 1992, p.139) zone imagined by Lacan where the body and its surroundings, inside and outside meet and coalesce. The tubular, concave, slippery objects turn us on, stimulating our sexuality into being, inviting desire and repulsion associated with bodily orifices. We want to grab, touch, caress or turn away in disgust. In turn, we feel watched and grabbed, teased and laughed at by these objects, seeming resistance to meaning and accessibility. Art and literature bring us closer to the fluttering states of our beginnings, where the boundaries between inside and outside, passivity and activity are murky. Through Kapoor's work, I want to show the inherent tensions in approaching the transsexual body as an enigmatic object. Confronting the obscurity of enigmatic objects returns us to the moment of emergence of our subjectivity where the interplay between experiences of pleasure and pain and presence and absence set our sexuality in transit and inaugurated the work of presentation. The elusive temporality mobilized by this strange and estranging encounter gives rise to conflicts around knowledge, love and truth. As we get closer to Kapoor's installations we may wonder: what is behind the object? Can we get inside it? What will I make from what I don't understand?

Art historian Henri Lustiger-Thaler (2010) describes Kapoor's abstract sculpture "Memory" in ways that illuminate the history of abstract art as an expressive form that attempts to represent the unrepresentable. "Memory" is an egg-shaped construction that is both heavy and hollow. It fills a room in the Guggenheim Museum in New York, yet it also gives the observer the impression that the underside of the capsule can be accessed through the narrow gaps on its sides. Lustiger-Thaler observes how the viewer is struck by the "purposeful inaccessibility" of the piece, because s/he cannot access the whole (2010, p. 17). Kapoor's giant capsule is simultaneously solid and hollow, certain in its concreteness and steadiness, yet deceptively empty. It is as certain as a vivid memory, a discernible screen-image that conceals its hollowness, distortions and necessary incompleteness. "Memory", Lustiger-Thaler suggests, "offers us a glimpse into the subterranean other side, where memory is still largely latent and imaginary" (2010, p. 17).

With its enigmatic hints, "Memory" compels us to "come in" only to be struck by an incomprehensible impossibility to access the piece. There is a limit to the visible image, forcing the onlooker to confront the void. Meaninglessness emerges as one tries to get a full grasp of the object, to situate it in time or history and to stabilize its meaning. As the spectator gets closer to Kapoor's "Memory", the solid materiality of the piece is revealed as imaginary and fleeting: the massive capsule is empty and its striking exterior hides an inaccessible underside. The observer finds herself caught between her desire to come closer, search and penetrate and her frustration at the structure's refusal to open itself and reveal its interior. Yet, in facing the enigma of "Memory", the onlooker may turn her anxiety over the opaqueness and impenetrability of the object into a devaluation of its undecipherable mystery: "a child could do it"; "it does not make sense". There is, I would argue, a certain correspondence between the transference provoked by these enigmatic encounters and the aesthetic conflict elicited in and through the child's interactions with the parental figure. An aesthetic crisis unfolds as our passion and hatred of knowledge converge. We attempt to both apprehend and repel the object that resists us with its inchoateness and estrangement.

As Lustiger-Thaler notes, the viewer of the giant piece is asked to ponder, "what remains concealed, and who is hidden and hence exiled to the invisible life of the Other?" (2010, p. 17). Through the insinuation of an access to the underside of the foreboding capsule that nevertheless remains elusive, the viewer is invited to "ponder the weight of the past within the memory" (Lustiger-Thaler, 2010, p. 17). The deceiving weight of the hollow structure that appears full propels a desire to return to the certainty of the image while simultaneously revealing the empty grounds on which the screen-image – that *is* memory – stands. Kapoor's sculpture is shaped in a way that captures the transitionality of memory, its suspension between "at least two compelling and defining moments" (Lustiger-Thaler, 2010, p.17), the primal moment of unconscious registration and the phantasy that structures this moment. The impossibility of memory, the inaccessibility that is suggested by Kapoor's piece, acts as a cut, a "third" immaterial space that mediates between what is and what can only be imagined. "Memory", like Kapoor's piece, "resists being viewed in its entirety" (Lustiger-Thaler, 2010, p. 18); memory will always be in excess of experience.

Poddar (2010) describes another of Kapoor's installations – an untitled work from 1975 that includes a chalk drawing of a hermaphrodite body connected to round and cubical geometric forms – as a "proto-body", a primal phantasy before "gendering and individuation" (p. 47). This primal representation depicts the body as a "cosmological entity having within it a picture of the universe" (Poddar, 2010, p. 47). The body, in other words, contains within itself an interior that mirrors its exterior. The installation also includes S-curved objects and hexagonal mirrors that "shatter and scatter the omnipotence of the gaze" (Poddar, 2010, p. 47), separating and conjoining interior and exterior. The ever-shifting distance between objects (appearing near and far, intermittently, through the fragmented mirror and the S-shaped metal capsule) evokes the timelessness of the unconscious and the instability of subjectivity. Seen as analytic objects, Kapoor's sculptures invite us to think of the outside as the nucleus of our interiority and ponder on the ways in which memory – itself a suspended, transitory space where "time and space have no real bearing" (Poddar, p. 49) – unites and separates internal and external reality, past and future. The "alien alterity" (Dean, 2000, p. 53) of the outside inhabits our innermost core. As Santner argues, it is on this paradox that the enigmatic character of human sexuality rests:

> What is generally thought to be the most animal-like about us – our sexuality – is, in this view, precisely where we are most out-of-joint with respect to any merely animal nature. We might say that, whereas instincts *orient,* our drive destiny, which emerges on the basis of our seduction by enigmatic signifiers – our "second birthday" – *disorients,* leading us along utterly and often painfully eccentric paths and detours. We are "driven", we have "drive destinies", because we find ourselves, at some level of our being, addicted to an always idiosyncratic series of enigmatic signifiers pertaining to the desire of the "big Others" in our lives. This also means that the most intimate kernel of our being is also what is most tightly linked to Otherness, though this link gets laid down below the level of intentionality and intersubjectivity proper.
>
> (Santner, 2005, p. 98)

Can observation of enigmatic art help us to sketch a theory of sexuality? Kapoor's art draws us to an undecipherable enigma by presenting the spectator with objects that resist comprehension and totalization, thus often leading to feelings of confusion, doubt, disorientation and helplessness. Many of Kapoor's pieces are reflective, mirror-like, as if they are observing the observer. These objects, in their fluid, shifty, undefined character, bring us closer to the underside of experience, the site of amnesia, endless questions and vacancy. We may think about our encounter with Kapoor's "Memory" in the same way that we think about our relationship to our own archival recollections: "Memory" reveals a fragmentation, a gap, that shatters the illusion of the object's completeness and of the subject's self-coherence. We are therefore reminded of the partiality of our relationship with reality, which always involves a brush against the "Real". In this way, the encounter with the enigmatic art object engages and mobilizes the polymorphous perversity of our desire because we cannot predict what is going to be made from this encounter.

The tension between fluidity and solidity, that is, the aporia of compact indefinition that "Memory" embodies, resonates with the tension inherent in the sexed body, a tension that is reanimated through the encounter with the transsexual body. The body, understood as both a psychic and material body, is also a bridge between the Real (impossibility), the Symbolic (Phantasy) and the Imaginary (concretization) and, therefore, a point of encounter between knowing and not knowing, life and death, finitude and infinity, satisfaction and difference. While it is commonly assumed that transsexuality implies a concretization of difference as enacted through surgery, I suggest that this very act of transitioning signifies an infinite quest, not a beginning nor an end, but a being-in-process, as one never arrives at a state of completeness. Transsexuality opens gender to its phantasy of cohesiveness and puts our notion of identity in transit. We are reminded here of the affective split described by Meltzer concerning our encounter with "reality" where objects arouse one emotion over another. We hate or love, we want to master or understand. However, when the object captivates us we "wish to ascertain its authenticity, to know it in depth. And at that moment, we encounter the heart of its mystery, along with the severe limitations in our capacity for knowledge" (Meltzer, 2008, pp. 143–144). Psychic transitioning becomes possible when the encounter with the object's enigma opens us and wounds us, when we become susceptible to their address.

Primal encounters

Before considering how gender functions as both a psychic object and state of mind, I need to put some ideas in place regarding the notion of aesthetic conflict as it occurs through the encounter with the enigma of art. Tackling the enigma of art through Kapoor's and Bourgeois' art pieces will allow us to consider the aesthetic flux that our encounter with enigmatic objects initiate, and in this context to examine gender as simultaneously an articulation of difference and a defense against it.

Thinking about art through Meltzer's notion of aesthetic conflict (2008), we can imagine Kapoor's "Memory" as a metaphor for the maternal body that stimulates and frustrates, calls forth sexuality and ambivalently elicits fantasies of plenitude and danger. Like the initial encounter with the maternal body, what registers as memory can only be constructed fragmentarily through our senses. Likewise, the observer of "Memory" feels pulled towards what seems hidden in Kapoor's monumental structure, resembling the process through which our sexuality is animated in the vicissitudes of maternal love. It is in this encounter, as Meltzer reminds us, that the desire to enter, possess and control that which cannot be seen emerges. The encounter with the enigmatic object/body is therefore also a confrontation with frustration, as the object/body resists our desire to domesticate its otherness, to placate that which distresses through care, to repudiate our feelings of vulnerability and dependency. The encounter with the maternal body is aesthetically conflicting because it inaugurates desire through imagination and doubt. It involves a conflict because the desire to know that it arouses is inseparable from experiencing the limitations of knowledge. What cannot be seen – the innards of the mother's body or her hidden genitals – creates anxiety and an always developing capacity to tolerate doubt, to wait and to be satisfied with fleeting experiences of love, truth and knowledge. Kapoor's opaque structure, like the maternal body, brings us into contact with momentary archaic jouissance, where the threat of fragmentation is joined with the thrill of merging. Kapoor's murky objects, which envelope us through their monumental size, simultaneously castrate us in luring us into its mysteries, making us lose our hold on reality, our awareness of time. We can either walk away and resist the enigma by walking away or we can ask: "If I change, what will I become?"

In a strikingly different artistic style, French-born artist Louise Bourgeois also captures phantasies of merging, incoherence, in-between spaces and the borderline zone between being and not-being, separation and joining. In stark contrast with Kapoor's monumental style, Bourgeois' pieces focus on the partial nature of objects, their smallness, malleability and effervescent quality: they seem compact yet elusive, passive yet forceful, resistant yet helpless. Often hanging in a suspended position, Bourgeois' pieces "change the hierarchy of the work; the base disappears" (Nixon & Bourgeois, 2005, p. 277). The objects are suspended – literally and figuratively – between phantasy and reality.

"Portrait"[2] (1963), for example, which is described by Deborah Wye (as cited in Nixon & Bourgeois, 2005, p. 188) as a "revolting" mass, makes us think of the body as a formless, undifferentiated body-object. Encountering Bourgeois' objects may provoke a transferential reaction of anxious identification with meaninglessness. Evoking womb-like, concave, hiding cavities, these objects capture the undifferentiated logic of the body and its finite character, which is expressed through fragmentation and degradation in which objects are reduced to undifferentiated matter. We may think of this "mess" as unsignified debris, as an excess that both castrates us and propels us into never-ceasing attempts at meaning making.

Lippard describes "Portrait" as "offensive" (as cited in Nixon & Bourgeois, 2005, p. 188). In general, she refers to Bourgeois' artwork as "transgressive" (as cited in Nixon & Bourgeois, 2005, p. 89) in its insistence on representing the uncontrollable drives with phallic imagery that nevertheless fails to contain them. In "Le Regard"[3] (1966), Bourgeois has the vagina looking at the viewer, pulling them to "its own level" (Nixon & Bourgeois, 2005, p. 167), the level of origin. Like the eye gazing through the anus in Bataille's famous novel *The Story of the Eye* (2001), the vagina engages our desire for abject knowledge – that which feels hidden, forbidden, simultaneously repelling and enticing. The sculpture is evocative in its erotic insinuations but sexually undifferentiated, inviting a visceral identification with a signifier that is both lacking and in excess.

Kapoor and Bourgeois are preoccupied with the enigma of embodiment, with its promise and failure to hold the promise of origin. In problematizing the body's seeming solidity and stability, their work reveals the precariousness of our signifying categories in the face of the body's inexhaustible inscrutability. Through their art, the penis, the breast and the womb are positioned as random, arbitrary objects, swinging to and fro, ambivalent and fleeting. When put to the test, their apparent "inner consistency" (Nixon & Bourgeois, 2005, p. 91) reveals itself as temporary and unstable.

One particular piece, Bourgeois' "Hanging Phallus"[4] (1968), seems to capture the way in which the penis – the ultimate marker of gender, the idealized object of certainty – is a "hanging" object, an object of suspense and uncertainty. "Hanging Phallus" de-symbolizes the penis and turns it into a hanger of sorts, in the sense that in its concreteness, it detains the polymorphous perverse movement of desire – its arbitrariness and unpredictability – thus preventing it from transitioning or shifting. This is reminiscent of the concept of "fetish" in that the presence of the phallic object reassures us of the seeming stability of sexual difference and provides us relief from the threat of ambiguity and self-difference. One can see how gender, perceived as a transparent binary categorization resting on a biological "truth", constitutes an example of fetishism, where the presence of the penis sets once and for all the question of sexual difference through the illusion of intelligibility. Despite our desire for phallic reassurance, for the stability that will take away the pain of ambiguity and ambivalence, we are haunted by the pulsating rhythm of the drive and the oscillation between pain and pleasure. In facing such vicissitudes of psychic life, the question of desire, and more specifically, of our peculiar position toward desire – what does it mean to be a man or a woman? – becomes an insisting address.

The imagination, which depends on psychic space, constitutes the register in which the obscure objects of the drive are retroactively signified and invested with meaning. In thinking of gender as an imaginary construction that articulates our phantasies of sexual difference within, outside and beyond the signifying structure of the symbolic order, gender identity becomes a collage of unconscious phantasies, both acted out and defended against, a site of trauma where what cannot be known, satisfied or settled appears as symptom or somatization, and simultaneously, as a fixed binary that halts desire. What is destroyed through the collapse of gender into a binary is the very otherness of gender, that is, gender as difference *within* the self. The idealization of the literal difference between the presence and absence of the penis and, with it, the concretization of gender as signifier that leads to 'object a' – the obscure object of desire – can be read in line with Bourgeois' depiction of the phallus: an obscene joke. If we are able to suspend this gigantic phallus, to dislodge it from its imaginary base, we can open it up to new resignifications through other, non-totalizing embodiments of desire. As a form of a phallic answer, the imaginary of gender can gag our desire, but not if "it" itself is understood as a gag.

Kapoor's "Memory" and Bourgeois' "Hanging Phallus" call forth an associative link between gender and memory as they relate to our theories of origin. Through her understanding of education as an encounter with an enigma that returns us to our childhood position as curious sexual researchers, Britzman (n.d.) reminds us that the "child researcher" grapples with questions such as "where did I come from?"; "where was I before I was born?"; "what would mommy and daddy do without me?" and "am I a boy or a girl?" These questions and their puzzling answers, which the child both embraces and resists, continue to pulse throughout our life despite the illusory certainties that the binary of gender provides us with. Kapoor's and Bourgeois' work helps us de-fuse the conflation between gender and desire, to reencounter anew the mystery of embodiment, and to release the fantasy of the body as origin and destiny.

Transsexuality as psychic space

In elaborating a link between the object of art and the sexed body it becomes clear that the aesthetic approach is ultimately a sexual one because it is predicated upon a relation to an enigmatic other who, given its structural self-decentredness, can never be fully known or apprehended. One implication of this approach is that it allows us to shift our conceptualization of transsexuality from a category that describes a particular sexual identity to a universal psychic position that allows sexuality to remain in a state of flux, always in transit. Indeed, the unfolding of psychic space depends upon the transsexuality of the psyche, that is, on its capacity to hold in tension ideality and enigma, drive and desire.

Shifting transsexuality from a diagnosis to a psychic position is not an easy task since it requires us to broaden our experience of sexuality by setting affect and thought in transit, away from the deadening fixity of identity. Both the aesthetic and the analytic encounters, insofar as they mobilize experiences of aesthetic conflict (Meltzer, 2008) that allow desire and creativity to emerge, constitute the holding ground for a reconceptualization of transsexuality as a psychic position.

To understand what it means to posit transsexuality as a psychic position, we need to address the relationship between the polymorphous perversity of the drives and the question of sexual difference, as well as how sexual difference is represented through the aesthetic conflict.

According to Freud, the drives are perverse because they are always partial, they do not have a preordained aim and are always amiss of the object. The demand of the drive is never fully satisfied because the condition for the absolute reduction of tension is death and so the drive undergoes a process of inhibition that paradoxically sustains desire. While Freud conceptualizes this inhibition as intrinsic to the drive because the drive's aim is death, the reduction of tension to zero; it is important to keep in mind that Freud posits this "death" as a "restoration of an earlier state of things" (1920, p. 37), that is, as an impossible return to a phantasized state of unity prior to the disruptive force of the drive. The satisfaction of the drive never culminates in this experience of self-coincidence, in fact, it pushes away from any form of stability as its aim is circumvented by the objects (*objet petit a*) it encounters on its way. As a bridge between desire and impossibility of satisfaction, the *objet petit a* simultaneously summons the drive and prevents it from reaching its aim.

In thinking through the aporia of the impossibility of the satisfaction of the drive, Bass (2006) comments on Freud's discussion of the relationship between the pleasure principle and the reality principle as theorized in *Beyond the Pleasure Principle* (1920). In this text, Freud proposes that "the reality principle allows the pleasure principle to reach its aim by more roundabout paths" (Bass, 2006, p. 140), which means, according to Bass, that there is no opposition between the two principles, but rather that the pleasure principle achieves its aim through delay and deferral, in short through *différance* (Derrida, 1982). In this new conceptualization, the other of pleasure, reality, becomes an inextricable aspect of itself.

The implications of this postulate can hardly be overstated, for as Bass argues, "Freud's description of how the pleasure principle defers its *self* through the reality principle illustrates how a differential, autoaffective structure lodges otherness within the self, the *autos*" (Bass, 2006, p. 140).

While it is usually understood as an unmediated form of satisfaction, the infant's experience with the breast already constitutes a registration of difference. Meltzer (2008) explains that for the infant, the breast or voice become objects of satisfaction – rather than means through which one can attain satisfaction – because the contents of the mother's body cannot be seen, controlled or appropriated. Partial erotogenic objects become transitional spaces that simultaneously bind and halt desire, thresholds that both connect and separate the infant and the mother, internal/external spaces. This, in Meltzer's view, constitutes the paradigmatic experience of aesthetic conflict, where the infant experiences the beauty of the mother's body precisely through its impossible appropriation at the moment when the "resolution" expected from satisfaction is most elusive. Meltzer's notion of the aesthetic conflict is tied to the polymorphous perversity of the drive, because the satisfaction of the drive depends on a compromise formation between the pleasure principle and the reality principle, between the drive's demand to return to an experience of primal satisfaction, which never existed prior to its loss, and the capacity to experience enjoyment, on condition that it is accepted as partial and temporary. As I have explained, it is in this aporetic space that the apprehension of beauty occurs and that psychic space is created.

Meltzer's notion of aesthetic conflict also helps us understand the way in which sexual difference is unthinkable without the polymorphous perversity of the drive because the drive's perversity implies a conflation of "subjective and objective sexual aims" (Bass, 2006, p. 130), self and other, life and death. As Bass suggests, Eros is "binding-differentiating" (2006, p. 129), where passivity and activity, masculinity and femininity are conflated. This conflation is a function of repetition because satisfaction is always displaced by the drive's push to return to a state of non-tension – a phantasied "earlier state of things" – and the impossibility of such return. Indeed, Freud's understanding of infantile sexuality as polymorphous–perverse establishes the accidental nature of gender identifications and the unpredictability of desire. Our sexuality does not know its destiny and is always in excess of identity. The perversity of the drive is psychoanalysis's fundamental insight into the essentially unstable and fragile nature of sexual identification, where the absence or presence of the penis is but a veil for a "deeper" irreducible absence at the level of the drives.

I stated before that the analytic encounter constitutes an experience of aesthetic conflict, which, by mobilizing our sexuality, destabilizes the subject's hold on the certainty of his identity. Indeed, the analytic act of losing and finding meaning is an imaginative experiment in holding on to the tension between pleasure and unpleasure. In analysis, sexual difference leaves the site of idealization to become the product of the analytic endeavour. De-idealization occurs bit by bit, through fragments of experiences that disappoint, miss or reveal the analyst as lacking.

It is a process of discovery in which the patient finds her own self-difference in her life-narrative, a difference that unsettles her relationship to her memories and decentres her imaginary sense of selfhood. The analytic encounter brings to light the way in which the imaginary of gender certainty and identification is tied, universally, to a whole constellation of childhood anxieties and repressed wishes. However, analysis also reveals the ways in which these elaborations are specific to each individual. It rewrites one's narrative through a new arrangement of screen memories, associations and signifiers and, therefore, through a re-shaping of object relations. At the end of the analytic process, according to Lacan, the subject emerges as "an individual without essence at all" (as cited in Johnston, 2005, p. 179).

Like an enigmatic art object, the analytic interpretation is not meant to explain or instruct, but rather to dislodge meaning, to evoke something primal, a wish for union, for absolute knowledge that is simultaneously circumvented through the inherent ambiguity of the work of interpretation that unsettles the subject's relation to the signifier. While recounting one's history involves a form of repetition, the "after education" of the analytic encounter ruptures the repetition, and through deferred action rearranges origin and genealogy in ways that often surprise us. The decentring force of interpretation often unsettles the subject's history of gender constitution, revealing the necessarily porous and partial quality of our sexual identifications and the unpredictable vicissitudes of desire.

Yet, psychoanalytic discourse cannot escape the trauma of its internal difference. Since Freud, psychoanalytic theory has oscillated between unfolding the fundamental thesis of the decentring power of sexuality, on which the existence of the unconscious is predicated, and its desire to settle the instability of the body of knowledge on which it relies. Psychoanalytic theories of gender identity that disavow the trauma of self-difference attempt to settle, through repetition and concretization, the enigma of sexuality by aligning itself with normative understandings of sexual embodiment. I have suggested that an aesthetic approach to transsexuality may produce repetition with difference through the Fort/Da of the analytic interpretation that revisits the site of trauma through new imaginative signifying paths.

In encountering the enigma of the analytic interpretation, we may come to think of our body not as a literal "truth" – nature-given and unambiguous – but instead, as a *literary* and *lateral* narrative: literary, insofar as the journey of embodiment is always in process and never fully decipherable; lateral insofar as it always unfolds in relation to other bodies as well as the subject's internal objects.

Sublimation, perversion and death

In this section I will address three seemingly unrelated concepts – sublimation, the death drive and perversion – in order to consider the question of gender embodiment as a process of self-reinvention.

I remind the reader that I use transsexuality as signifier, rather than as a diagnosis or destination, that takes different meanings at different times. It refers to the essentially unstable and fragile nature of sexual identification, since our sexuality, in its effervescent quality, is traversed by the unconscious and as such it always threatens intelligibility. However, transsexuality also refers to the capacity to rest on partial objects, to capture enjoyment through transitory moments in time.

Seen through the lens of perversion, mainstream psychoanalytic theory has aligned transsexuality with static non-transitionality, symbolic equation, fetishizing and omnipotent control over the body. However, Freud's understanding of the drive makes perversion an inherent quality of the drive insofar as its object is neither predetermined nor fully satisfactory. Understood as a limit-concept between soma and psyche, the drive and its vicissitudes cannot be understood outside of the subject's relation to the signifier and, therefore, to culture. While culture shapes our relation to the signifier, the subject is formed both in excess and in lack in relation to these signifying relationships. In this context, the polymorphous perversity of the drive aligns with non-conformity, with the subject's capacity to play with the signifier in ways that escape the determinisms of culture. Perversion, therefore, speaks essentially about the subject's capacity to transgress and shape the signifier.

Copjec further elaborates the relation between drive and perversion as initially articulated by Freud. The drive, she writes, "does not finish so easily with its object, but keeps turning around it" (2004, p. 38). Like the pervert, the drive derives satisfaction from never reaching the object, from circling around it. Here, sublimation is brought closer to perversion, because "sublimation is a consequence of the potentially endless displaceability of the drive from any particular or given context, aim, or object" (Grosz, 2001, p. 144). Both in perversion and in sublimation, the object is brushed against, circumvented, played with. In this understanding of sublimation, the relation to enjoyment can be described as perverse, if we use the term to describe the differing and differentiating aspects of this "endless displaceability".

In attempting to triangulate perversion, sublimation and the death drive in order to think the process of gender embodiment as transitioning, I will follow Copjec's elaboration of the connection between death and sublimation. Copjec (2004) reminds us that the notion of death in psychoanalysis is a metaphoric rather than a literal concept that refers to the drive's search for a mythical state of fullness, when subject and object are not yet divided, a state that never existed prior to its loss. The drive's aim towards death is therefore "what we can only regard as potential immortality" (Freud, 1920, p. 40).

From this perspective, Copjec stresses, the body is finite only if we assume a point of transcendence, that is, of ultimate satisfaction, but the body in psychoanalysis is a sexual body and as such is infinite, forever yearning, desiring, for the drive never achieves its aim. The object of desire, which summons the drive, is also that which "breaks the drive" and "divides it into partial drives" (Copjec, 2004, p. 34), thus making all experiences of satisfaction transient and fragmentary. These partial drives find transitory resting places, "small nothings" (Copjec, 2004, p. 34), which satisfy without the drive ever attaining its aim. This paradox, the idea that the drive is satisfied "through its being thwarted" (Grozs, 2001, p. 132), is explained by the fact that the drive's aim is really to return to this circuit, that enjoyment lies precisely in this circling around the object of desire.

From here it follows, as Copjec reminds us, that sublimation, the inhibition of satisfaction, is "the proper destiny of the drive" (2004, p. 30). In other words, if the only potential for satisfaction lies in these experiences of partial satisfaction, then satisfaction relies upon deferral, on the endless postponement inherent in the drive's pursuit of enjoyment.

If death in psychoanalysis coincides with infinity – a phantasized state of wholeness and plenitude – the aim of the death-drive can only be endless deferral. Paradoxically, this is also the very condition for self-redefinition. The impossibility of wholeness means the inevitability of a remainder, of an excess that produces self-estrangement from oneself and pushes for self-invention. The oscillation between the death drive's thrust to "return" to a primordial time of non-differentiation, on the one hand, and the perpetual demand for "work" sustained by the impossibility of satisfaction, on the other, brings us back to the possibility of psychic transitioning as a means to embody this irreducible tension, to "reincarnate" (Copjec, 2004, p. 51) this difference through investment in partial objects. We give body to our libido through erotogenic small objects (Copjec, 2004, p. 51) such as the penis, vagina and mouth.

Copjec's formulation of sublimation as the body's capacity to "reincarnate what is other to it" (2004, p.51) suggests that sublimation is a transitional state that is linked with an aesthetic conflict where partial objects act as a compromise formation between absence and presence, inside and outside, separation and union. Here sublimation is linked with the pleasure we obtain from "objects of lack" – *petit a* – which, in their partiality and transient nature, remind us of the impossibility of absolute jouissance or of transcending the fundamental self-difference that defines the subject. Thinking of gender in relation to sublimation it is possible to see how *engenderment* – a word that evokes both gender and origin – alludes to the ways in which "coming to gender" involves a re-invention of the body as a fragmentary, limited, and finite object, hence as a psychic body governed by the aesthetic conflict.

The body in psychoanalysis is a sexual one and therefore, a relational body that interacts with and is affected by other bodies, that takes other bodies as its own and that finds its own corporal experience through its relation to others. Copjec's (2004) understanding of the body as a psychic object and hence, as a phantasy object, helps us reformulate gender identity as a tenuous achievement. Engenderment relates to sublimation because this process involves the ability to enjoy the lacking, incomplete body, the body in process. Considered in this way, gender can function as a transitional object or as fetish. Like the fetish, gender cannot be given up; however, like a transitional object, it provides an intermediate area of experience between discovery and creation, between subjective and shared experience. As a transitional object, gender occupies an intermediate space between the imaginary, symbolic and the real, in which erotogenic objects become interchangeable and where the phallus functions as a bridge, which could both deny and affirm sexual difference. The sexed body marks a concrete split (male/female) that covers over what is invisible in the body, its opacity and internal movements. Through the imaginary of gender, we signify the sexed body as an object of certainty and idealization where the phallus – as a signifier of completeness and intelligibility – hangs, leading us to 'object a': the obscure object of desire.

While thinking the transsexual body as a metaphor for the state of mind on which sublimation depends, it is important to remember that the body is not simply a creation of the psyche. Gender functions as a phantasy; it is enjoyed as an object of certainty, but gender is also linked to the real of sexual difference. We can never fully know the object of our desire; we never know our gender and we can never cease to ask: "Am I a man or a woman?" However, approaching the real of sexual difference as destiny, as the truth of engenderment, delivers the body to tyranny. Through analysis, on the other hand, the psyche can be opened to the enigma of engenderment by linking the specificity of the unconscious to the social imaginary through sublimation: between discovery and self-creation.

While "transitioning" is a process that belongs quintessentially to the transsexual subject whose process of "becoming other" is marked on the body, the motif of transitioning, however, is universal and it involves a crisis that puts in flux our history and destiny. For the psyche, transitioning occurs on the plain of phantasy because it engages the history of our object relations, which are always partial, transient and unconscious. We can never know the other to whom we relate or the other's desire. This fundamental estrangement from the other – which inaugurates our own estrangement from ourselves – marks our history as discontinuous, fragmented and relative. As Proust (2001) reminds us, history can only be regained through tentative attempts at piecing together, from fleeting memories, a narrative that can only provide us with momentary clarity. Regaining our history requires reinventing our origins.

The art of sublimation

The tenuous link between reality and phantasy that turns objects into psychic placeholders is articulated by Poddar's keen observation about Kapoor's art. Poddar observes how Kapoor's sculpture "Memory" is "de-materialized" (2010, p. 28) despite being made of steel, because it cannot be grasped by the observer as whole and so its intelligibility is broken down by its incommensurability. Kapoor, Poddar suggests, is successful in "sacrificing the status of the object" by creating an effect where the observer is "bound between abject beauty and terror" (Poddar, 2010, p. 28). "Memory" registers a limit to our awareness. As we try to "overcome memory's constraint" we become "even more aware of our own body" (Poddar, 2010, p. 28) and, we may add, its psychical constraints. Remembering is both an act of retrieval and loss, for the screen of memory reveals as much as it conceals. Poddar's engagement with Kapoor's art helps us think of embodiment as a holding place where, like Kapoor's sculpture "matter and memory together embody the simultaneity of the experiential and imagined world" (Poddar, 2010, p.28). Like Kapoor's sculpture – tenuous, opaque, not fully graspable – the body "exceeds somatic comprehension" (Poddar, 2010, p. 28).

The transsexual body animates this inapprehensibility since, not unlike Kapoor's objects, it unsettles the viewer's very concept of gender as known, recognizable and whole. When one accepts the enigmatic nature of the transsexual body, that is, without disavowing its disruption of the continuity between sex and gender, it necessarily calls into question our own hold on our gendered identity as it asks us to sacrifice our own stake in its imaginary objectivity. Thinking of gender through art reveals how this imaginary construction contains a trace of unconscious desire that is irreducible to the social, cultural, or historical determinants of sexual identity. This process dismantles the idealization that sustains our loyalty to the impersonal Other (i.e. culture) understood as an essential, necessary and timeless symbolic ordering of subjectivity.

Why, as Poddar suggests, is sacrificing the object a "success"? Kapoor's objects help us consider the link between memory and embodiment as fragile and tenuous. If our bodies are shaped by memory's constraints, and memory is subject to the body's excess (sexuality), then the process of coming to gender becomes an experience made of the conflicted encounter between phantasy and matter. From this perspective, it could be said that the work of phantasy fulfills the function of symbolizing this misencounter through an individual theory of origin that narrates the process of our becoming gendered.

Psychoanalytic theory reminds us that subjectivity rests on the loss of an imagined cohesiveness that only exists as a retroactively constructed phantasy. The endless search for the object that would finally return us to this state of undividedness, of absolute presence, drives the subject's investment in the object of desire: always amiss, always unattainable. As "memory" suggests, it is a lost piece that is veiled by its visible fragments. Kapoor's "Memory", like the analytic narrative, does not represent the object of memory but rather the imaginary link between a mnemic construction and the raw gash of the subject's structural lack. Like the object of art, gender can be transformed into a soft, plastic object that can be played with, but only if this object of "the Real" is "sacrificed" and turned into an object of the imagination.

Perhaps if we imagine the Fort/Da of the narrative of gender through the constrains of body and memory we may also come to understand the course of embodiment, its (im)possibility, as other than an appeal for recognition of trauma; that is, as a relation to the body that is not fully governed by identification. But what would it mean to think of gender without the idealized other? Here, Pluth's (2007) interpretation of the Fort/Da game as an act that reconfigures the mother's departure as a cause for desire may be illuminating. Indeed, rather than an attempt to bring back the absent mother or to mourn her loss, the Fort/Da game would constitute, in this reading, an exercise on the process of substitution itself. In this sense the Fort/Da game is an act of engenderment insofar as it becomes the means through which one comes to terms with the otherness of the other and situates oneself in relation to this other and his/her desire. Like the spectator's relation to art, it involves a narrative that leaves space for the unrepresentable, the unknown, and the unintelligible while simultaneously allowing the subject to locate herself into a narrative that both precedes and exceeds her.

By tying memory to the unknown and unknowable, the Fort/Da of gender leaves the site of memory as certainty to bring back, in a Proustian move, a novel. Turning the narrative of transsexuality to novel means changing our understanding of what it means to be gendered in a way that returns meaning to its vacancy. While the subject's discourse cannot escape trauma, neither the structural nor the contingent, the process of gender resignification offers us the possibility of constructing contingent and transitory links between the timelessness of trauma and the concretizing response of conscious time. In analysis this narrative takes the shape of a Fort/Da, always failing to settle while becoming itself the very tension it attempts to resolve. The differing and deferring qualities of interpretation turn the analysand's demand into an address; a communication to an unknown other, which cannot elicit a foreseeable response. It is through this declaration that "something is" (2007, p. 104), which, according to Ed Pluth, defines the use of signifiers in the Fort/Da, that something other comes to be in the moment of transition, in the tension between Fort and Da. While the enigma of interpretation brings about the omnipotent desire constitutive of the Fort/Da – to bring the mother back – it also elicits its failure. It is a call for the imagination to open up the subject's narrative to the irreducible discontinuity of the subject's history.

We have come to conceive of the gendered body as an image that conceals an unknown, a riddle, and also as an imaginary construction that attempts to give shape to, as it dismantles in this very act, the source or nature of one's desire. Encountering enigma, paradox and confusion is traumatic for the subject who may succumb to the demand for a phallic response that in replacing thinking with omnipotent knowledge manages to stop time. In the analytic setting, while the attribution of knowledge to the analyst – the subject supposed to know – inaugurates the transference, this positioning of the analyst as a phallic object must ultimately reveal itself as illusory as the analyst progressively becomes the object through which the analysand invest in the analytical process itself as a transitional space. The analyst's refusal to occupy the position of mastery replaces the patient's quest for a hidden truth into a search for the truth of enigma, which functions as placeholder for future longing and temporary enjoyment.

If on the social level transsexuality implies both a wish to become other than oneself and an embodiment that is marked as other, understood as a psychic position, transsexuality is akin to the analytic ethos that invites the patient to dwell in transitionality, in the back and forth of the Fort/Da. While sex reassignment surgery may be in some cases motivated by the omnipotent wish to arrive at the desired gender and as such, it may connote a concretization of difference, the very act of transitioning also signifies an infinite quest, as one never arrives at a state of completeness. As a concept that implies both a peculiar form of embodiment and the polymorphousness of desire, transsexuality illuminates both the risks and the potential of every gendered formation while simultaneously revealing "the symptom" that is gender.

The Fort/Da of the analytic transference repeats the "transsexual" rhythm of time by placing sexuality always in relation to past, present and future. The enigmatic nature of interpretation opens up a space between time and timelessness, certainty and confusion, passivity and activity, repeating this transit quality of sexuality. Between the desire for dedifferentiation (Bass, 2000) – the wish to remain embedded in an all-embracing totality – and a curiosity that gains impetus through the analytic relationship, the work of interpretation moves the patient through a signifying repetition that is binding–differentiating yet non-persecutory. It transforms thought into an object for inquiry and attempts to introduce flexibility and ambiguity in an environment that is structured as reliable through its temporality: it is both unpredictable and stable. Psychoanalysis, therefore, commits us to an act of differing and deferring repetition, pushing us to look again and again in displaced, retroactive fashion, for the lost object that can never be re-found. The emptiness of gender makes the question of origin one of simulacrum, displacement and construction: artwork. Creating an origin through the narrative of analysis is an act of doubling that paradoxically "gathers the subject together" through separation and difference.

If analysis involves an inherently unsettling inquiry into the virtual nature of our archive, and if, as Freud suggests, sexuality is linked with memory through a psychic act of deferral, then it could be argued that analytic discourse is inherently transsexual. Through the act of interpretation, our desire is set in constant transit in a terrain of diverse temporalities, between sensual and conceptual forms of experience. Analysis returns us to a helpless state; it is, in a way, a traumatic configuration that returns us to a time of susceptibility, which animates as it inaugurates our fate. What would it mean to carve a solution to the aesthetic conflict proposed by the analytic encounter? To the uncertainty of psychic life? In the next chapter I will turn to literature as a way to articulate contrasting approaches to the gender question understood as aesthetic conflict.

Notes

1 http://slamxhype.com/art-design/anish-kapoor-memory-instillation/
2 http://www.moma.org/collection/object.php?object_id=81415
3 http://www.flickr.com/photos/51845767@N05/4984003640/
4 http://www.flickr.com/photos/centralasian/8120315497

Chapter 3

Narrating transsexuality
Transition from memoir to literature

> *And almost a girl it was who was born from this*
> *happy union of song and lyre and gleamed clearly*
> *through her springtime veils and made herself a bed in my*
> *ear.*
>
> From "And almost a girl it was",
> Rainer Maria Rilke

When thinking of the intrigue of the sexual body in the last century, two literary characters and two different solutions to the question "am I a boy or a girl?" come to mind: Foucault's (1980) *Herculine Barbin* and Eugenides' character Calliope ("Cal") from the novel *Middlesex* (2002). We know of Herculine through Michel Foucault's publishing of her diary in 1980. She was a hermaphrodite living in France from 1830 to 1860, attending an all-girls school who committed suicide at the age of 30. Living in different times and contexts, Calliope's and Herculine's complex theories of origin and becoming represent two different ways of constructing gender and the phantasized Other. Both provide the possibility of writing the sexual body, both capture the phantasies of intersex and transsexuality circulating then and now in the public imaginary, and both of their narratives touch upon a collapse of meaning, forms of madness and notions of transformation. And yet, the narrative of their gender embodiment is strikingly different.

As enigma, gender presents as riddle: "am I a boy or a girl?" In considering the interface between body and language we face a choice. Can our narrative be of one gender and our body of another? What is entailed in such a choice? Our characters present us with two different answers to the question of gender, one that is embedded in the social and another where desire becomes a differentiating compass.

It is therefore tempting to be preoccupied with questions of cultural discourse as the experience of gender and the possibility of change are so thoroughly scripted. Indeed, the impact of historical time cannot be denied because the signifiers of gender that were available to Herculine are fewer than those available to Eugenides, though for each, language brings them to their limit. Herculine's diary and Eugenides' novel – written as an adolescent memoir – allow us glimpses into our own hallucinations of gender: we too are thoroughly embedded in our theories of origin. We too hope that the phantasized Other will guarantee meaning.

Before we enter into the question of gender, let us pause for a moment to consider the move from visual art to literature. Literature allows us to treat characters as analytic objects. When we treat objects analytically we observe our own observations. Psychoanalysis teaches us that we are *affected* before we understand and that consciousness is always fragmentary, and discontinuous. Literature allows us to take our time to observe the machinations of our own understanding. We are allowed to separate from our objects, slowly take distance from them, and treat them softly as malleable and transitional objects.

It is particularly difficult to dislodge transsexuality from its known meaning, to consider it as a transitional object and as a question of object relations. A move toward the literary will help us make this gradual shift from understanding the body as an object of certainty to encounter it as a site of enigmas. The difference between literature and the clinic is that in the act of reading the reader becomes the analysand: always in her mind, experiencing the novel as a riddle, as an enigma that puzzles. Much like in the analytic process, where the objects handed over to the analyst seem gigantic and obscure, our reading may provoke a sense of confusion that will entice us to leave our certainties behind.

By turning to the novel, I wish to examine *novel* ways in which sexuality and gender unfold and to explore how, through resisting and revealing assumed origins, we learn more from our fragile attempts to settle desire. Like fiction, gender hints at trauma that has no origin because it is the result of the struggle to capture an unknown, which can only be brushed against. One cannot enter the novel's narrative armed with the "right" knowledge to grasp its meaning. One is affected by the novel's aftershock. One cannot prepare for sexuality's novelty, and its meanings can only be found retroactively, only after desire surprises, strays us from familiar courses and forces an engagement with the open question of identity. An analytic reading of the novel will pay attention to the character's attempt to find creative solutions to the questions that plague her but also to those occasions when this is not possible. If we were to engage with the novel analytically, how might we listen to the characters? What does the analyst listen to and for? These are the questions that I am bringing in understanding transitioning in relation to desire and to the subject's capacity to re-read and re-write the body.

Readers may find it confusing to be acquainted with Calliope and Herculin Barbin, who are described as intersex, in a study of transsexuality. I have decided to use the intersex body because it brings the incommensurability between sexuality and gender to the fore. The intersex body, it can be argued, exceeds somatic conceptualization of gender identity because, by definition, genitalia is not a defining criteria for sexual identity. Furthermore, the intersex body draws attention to the act of seeing as sustaining the mystery of the body's intelligibility.

Truth or dare: adolescent stories of origin

In his introduction to Herculine Barbin's memoir, Foucault (1980) describes how, with the rise of the post-Renaissance medical discourse, the question of the intersex condition turned from a matter of gender choice to one of law – of establishing "true sex" (Foucault, 1980, p. xi). Establishing the legitimacy of one's sex also opened the possibilities of deception and transgression, uniting knowledge and nature in a peculiar bond. In relation to intersex, this link between knowledge and nature is evident in the assumption that one's "true sex" is hidden behind anatomical oddities. The concern here is with "dissembling" (Foucault, 1980, p. ix) the intersex subject's inmost knowledge in order to gain access to her "true" sex.

Foucault describes the relationship between sex and truth in psychoanalytic discourse according to which "we must not deceive ourselves concerning our sex, [for] our sex harbors what is most true in ourselves" (Foucault, 1980, p. xi). Establishing the legitimacy of sexual constitution became a sort of guard against deception – the possibility for some individuals to transgress "natural law" and deceive others by presenting as the "other sex". His introduction to Herculine's memoir raises the problem of our passion for origin (the cause that causes every cause) as it relates to our desire to stabilize the self through cause. I am lead to ask, can psychoanalysis open the transference to the infinite irresolvability of gender?

The question of truth and sexuality becomes a particular preoccupation in the narratives of the adolescents Calliope and Barbin. Herculine's memoir and *Middlesex* represent two ways in which truth and sex intersect. In both texts, the characters are not the authors of their gender, at least not initially. It is a granting authority, a doctor, a parent or a schoolmaster, that decides the child's sex, based, as Foucault reminds us, on the pursuit of a "true sex" that is "hidden beneath ambiguous appearances" (1980, p.viii). The pursuit of "true sex", for both Calliope and Herculine, does not ensue until puberty, when an encounter with a gaze of the all-knowing Other – the clinic, the doctor, the school, the parents – seems to divert desire from its polymorphous course and force it to turn it against itself. No longer is there permission to enjoy the "limbo of non-identity" (Foucault, 1980, p. xiii). It is at this point that each character's narrative begins.

Each character presents a narrative of their phantasized history. In the act of recounting their history, memory and forgetting come close. We encounter adolescent passion, nostalgia, ideality and phantasized primal scenes. Forgetting becomes a form of remembering, as manifested in the hiatuses between telling and not telling, knowing and not knowing. As each character recounts her or his retrospective weaving of events, readers come to wonder how their attempt to reconstruct origin from fragments of memories helps perpetuate or obstruct desire. Reading Herculine's memoir and Eugenides' novel we may wonder if narrative can be read as memory. Freud reminds us that a successful history is always forgotten and memories carry the enigma of sexuality. An attempt to recapture what has been lost in time together with the failure to remember is the paradox of narrative.

We witness in *Middlesex* (Eugenides, 2002) the close connection between memory and imagination when Calliope (Cal) says: "I was born twice, once as a baby girl, on a remarkably smogless day in January 1960; and then again, as a teenage boy; in an emergency room near Petoskey, Michigan, in August of 1974"

(Eugenides, 2002, p. 3). The "second birth" occurs as Cal is rushed to the hospital following an "accident" and where her enigmatic sexuality is discovered, causing "confusion". For Calliope, we learn, re-birth is tightly bound with confusion: the confusion on the doctor's face upon discovering Calliope's ambiguous genitalia, the confusion of her parents upon being given the news that their daughter is a boy and finally Calliope's own confusion.

Because of the enigmatic nature of his/her history, Cal is a labile subject that can fall on either side, as a man or as a woman. The confusion reflected in the doctor's and Cal's parents' faces and speech mirrors Calliope's confusion, a riddle that could be solved if she only looks "closely enough". The examination in the emergency room opens Cal to the enigma of her body and sets her on a journey in search of identity. Through *Middlesex,* we accompany Calliope's retrospective search of her origin in the "accident" that can explain her gender dis-order, only to find ourselves at the beginning of the story, now retold by Cal. Calliope's time travel is made through Eugenides' writing and so *Middlesex* opens an enigma for the readers: can writing be an act of re-birth? What kind of a novel would we have to write that would re-write us?

Cal's memories of origin spread across three generations. These memories are testimonies to the ways in which gender originates as well as explanations of the origins of identity – whether they are genes, socialization or fantasies of the primal scene. Her attempt to settle gender through recourse to origin, however, falls apart: when Calliope was a little girl, s/he was a little boy. The question of gender cannot be settled through the search for origin.

Cal's story of origin becomes a configuration of the oedipal drama through a primal scene involving incest. His grandparents, a brother and a sister, were unable to comprehend or resist their desire. They fall in love and eventually marry. It is a story of transgression invented as cause for his "accident of gender" (Gozlan, 2008). Their strange union is phantasized as the origin of Calliope's genetic accident, which is really a denial of other accidents: the accidental desire of the brother and sister in the absence of a prohibiting parent and the accident of gender itself that is always lacking in origin and is always a lack. The lack also installs another prohibition: the phantastic incestuous union of Calliope's grandparents betrays desire, which can only be born of unpredictability. There is a desperate insistence in their wanting.

It is difficult to describe intersex Calliope without getting caught in the unintelligibility of gender. Calliope's narrative produces mixed emotions and perplexes our fragile hold on gender. As readers, we struggle throughout the book with the question of where to situate Calliope in gender. We may attempt to force Calliope into a gender position, acting out our own projection. Situating Calliope in gender seems inevitable and urgent. Are we transferentially captured by Calliope's illegible experience or by our own anxiety of meeting our own illegible gender? Calliope's narrative and the reader's struggle with gender positioning reflect the difficulty of thinking about gender without recourse to an origin story. As our character struggles with what is experienced as an enigmatic history handed down through the generations, the question for the reader becomes, what meaning can we make from our own "accident of gender"?

The question of meaning and sexuality is one invoked by Freud, when he insists on the paradox of sexuality that is beyond meaning: "it goes lower and also higher than its popular sense" (Freud, 1910, pp. 221–222). The paradox of sexuality is that it is predicated upon lack. To be sexual we must continue making meaning but we must also be duped by the meaning we make rather than become absorbed in its literality. Like the drive, we must miss our own aim, we must fail to attain the object of desire. By definition, sexuality is a violation of doxa: it is transgressive and rules out normalcy. In Freud's perspective, the sexed body feels propelled to unite with an external object that will gratify all its needs but the drive can only circumvent the object and find temporary satisfaction.

The transsexual and intersex bodies seem to literalize the complex relationship between sexuality and meaning: they transgress stable theories of origin at the same time as they desire certification from the other. Such dilemma confirms the way in which our sexuality depends on the Other, an Other that both exhilarates and terrifies, permits and prohibits. Cal's fight with desire may help us understand the transsexual patient's need to seek comfort in a fantasy of "settled" gender; it may also broaden the dilemma of gender as a human condition, not limited to the transsexual position.

The reader of *Middlesex* may also identify with Cal's urgency to settle the question of identity. Through the novel, we are confronted with trauma: there is never complete knowledge of oneself, there is never a complete gender or a normal self. Instability is a precondition for desire, relying as it does on incompleteness, suspense and yearning. We come to see every body as a hysterical body, a body signified in the Other's terms.

Unlike Eugenides' novel, which starts with a re-birth, Herculine Barbin's memoir begins with a proclamation of death and despair: "I am beyond doubt approaching the hour of my death . . . forsaken by everyone!" (Foucault, 1980, p. 3). Herculine, as Foucault describes, "left (her) childhood only to draw apart from the world, condemned, by the strangeness of her body, to live as stranger" (1980, p. 3). We learn, however, that there is a precursor to this estrangement associated with the entrance into adolescence. We also learn that she never knew her father and, by age of seven, had been given away by her mother. In fact, Herculine's memoir can be read as a relentless search for a lost mother. The maternal space is replaced by other maternal figures from which Herculine derives passive pleasure. Living in girls' schools and convents, she experiences the pleasure of being touched by words of the mother superior, taken into the homes of the nuns or under their "wings", kissed and caressed, being "gazed" at (Foucault, 1980, p. 5). "The mother" plays a dominant role in the narrative despite the fact that she is barely mentioned or remembered. She is found in the teachers, the mother superior and finally her supervisor at the convent, who enacts an uncanny repetition of Herculine's history when she sends her away upon discovering her "true" gender. The search for the mother culminates in yet another abandonment from which Herculine never recovers. And yet there is her testimony.

The convent experience is described by Herculine as a transitional womb-like space that permits ambiguity, an intermediate, safe space, where Herculine can hold on to the enigma of gender. She presents as a woman with masculine features, she is tender and educated, a writer and a schoolmaster, all contradictory terms, in Herculine's time. The convent is a place where sexuality is atmospheric, both absent and intensely present. Herculine writes of being shaken by "tumultuous feelings" (Foucault, 1980, p. 39) as she watches the "carefree" girls and the "infinitely superior" (Foucault, 1980, p. 43) beauty of her teachers. She describes her days as a girl as "the fine days of a life" (Foucault, 1980, p. 87) but, in retrospect, she feels "doomed to abandonment, to cold isolation" (Foucault, 1980, p. 87). Being declared a man by a priest and a doctor, Herculine is sent away from the convent. It marks a paradoxical moment where, all at once, she receives the desired certitude that will settle her nagging ambiguity but the certitude itself is unbearable. Why, we may ask, does the point of recognition become the time when Herculine kills herself? What was foreclosed by the literalization of gender?

The imminence of death is present at the very beginning of Herculine's narrative where she declares, "I am beyond doubt approaching the hour of my death" (p. 3). Barbin destroys herself through suicide, and leaves us a memoir that is written as a nostalgic pining for a time lost to transition:

> Not a living creature was to share in this immense sorrow that seized me when I left my childhood, at that age when everything is beautiful, because everything is young and bright with the future. That age did not exist for me. As soon as I reached that age, I instinctively drew apart from the world, as if I had already come to understand that I was to live in it as a stranger.
> (Foucault, 1980, p. 3)

Herculine's memoir, like Calliope's narrative, addresses the history of her transgression: a genetic mistake, an error of nature that "baffles every possible attempt to make an identification" (Foucault, 1980, p. xii). Her adolescence is marked by the trauma of gender where bodily changes shatter the "happy limbo of a nonidentity" (Foucault, 1980, p. xiii). Something has gone awry. The certainty of identification had shaken the coordinates of time, turning mute objects to speaking subjects. But the speaking subject is also baffled. We may wonder: why did an answer to her bafflement render her mute?

We can imagine a series of events that leave a mark on Herculine's embodied memory: the mother's enigmatic message, her possible handling of her "strange" child, and her abandonment: All joined in a particular way to mark what becomes Herculine's body. Is there jouissance in Herculine's search for her lost mother? And what happens to this search, to this jouissance, when she is declared a man?

We can read Herculine's melancholy reminiscence as an attempt to give meaning to a difficult past that creates a mesmerizing mythology of youth. She describes her adolescent years in the convent as happy times when she enjoyed her "girliness" but also as times where she finds fleeting pleasures in the strange embodiment that separates her from other girls. Being declared a man through a medical examination, which reveals a "hidden" male organ, brings about a second abandonment. Herculine's gender has been literalized in a culture where the enigma of gender is foreclosed; this cultural foreclosure is repeated in the fixity of the writing, where the literal cannot become literary.

For Herculine, the indeterminacy of her sex was constructed as monstrosity, thus exposing a phantasy of origin that views sex as essence. It is as if the history of her gender came, abruptly and violently, from without, fixating her in an impossible position in which she could never be recognized, in which she did not know how to be. But there is an incessant repetition, a search for maternal acceptance, a playing out of abjection and abandonment that exceeds her circumstances and that "forbids the emergence of an outside of history" (Copjec, 2004, p. 96). Something in Herculine resisted transformation; she could not imagine herself in transition. She could not ask herself: am I a man or woman? There is no revolt in her memoir, just a passive compliance with the conventional imaginary.

The place of separation from the Other is refused and her pleasure remains tied to a lost world that both enchants and estranges. The unattainable objects she encounters melt away with each memory recounted. The memoir itself becomes a bottomless pit of memories that fix her in a place she is not: away from her present. Perhaps the place of estrangement was the only space that enlivened Herculine, a place where she was neither alive nor dead. But she is unable to fight the abjection of interpellation, to set the Other aside. Does the literalization of her identity and desire foreclose all possibility of a return to this enigmatic state where she could hold her mother as both present and absent?

Herculine Barbin and *Middlesex* present us with two ways of relating to "lost time" before gender presents itself as dilemma, a process each character attempts to re-capture through writing. For Calliope the re-write, which is also a re-birth, happens at the point of arrival. Cal arrives at a point where he can re-write his body. In the process of re-telling, Cal's memory is fractured and made into something else, an unknown that he must "read it from the beginning to get to the end" (Eugenides, 2002, p. 20).

Herculine and Calliope invite the reader to learn about binding and unbinding through their narratives of desire and disappointment, through their attempts and failures at living their predicament creatively. Herculine's nostalgic narrative about her life before the certainty of gender reads like an adolescent novel, saturated with longing and desperation for the unattainable – a struggle with adolescence, and a resistance to leave youth behind. The narrative is infused with a belief that is common to many transsexual appeals: a conviction that the paradise of the complete body is indeed within reach, if only one possesses the "right" body, the body that captures and is captured by the desire of the Other. Possession of the "right" body is also a wish for certainty; but certainty, as Adam Phillips (2013) reminds us, is also a misrecognition, a necessary form of escape "required to construct an acceptable image of oneself" (p. 129). Knowledge becomes an escape from the uncertainty of what one wants, from the uncertainty of desire. After being declared to be male, Herculine is certain of her gender. Certainty becomes an escape from the uncertainty of love, and death becomes the only guarantee that she will not be abandoned.

Herculine's memoir shows us the close connection between the body and knowledge when she describes the unknown as something that always leads to sadness and feels like "sickness". Indeed our bodies are always bodies of knowledge that require interpretation. This strange "unknown" hints at the memoir's other side – the inaccessibility, ambiguity and ambivalence of memory. As we read Herculine's memoir we are left with a question: what is it that the writing covers up that is then transferred to the reader? Who is the Other within the self that is excluded from memory/memoir? These questions link the body, as a body of work (writing, art), with the Other, and in this way, the body, like writing or art, also becomes a carrier of what is not remembered, a "mystic writing pad" (Freud, 1925). If the body carries a trace of inevitable traumatic loss, it also becomes a site of the incomprehensible, of the invisible, that frightens, like the infinity of death. Can the enigma of Herculine's body capture her inscribed phantasies of a rejecting womb? Can Herculine's suicide be read as an escape from symbolization, from uncertainty? What is it that misrecognition could not escape?

Adolescent belief

Herculine, we must remember, is an adolescent and the adolescent believes in gender. In her paper on "Adolescence: A syndrome of ideality", Kristeva (2007) notes how refusal of loss places the subject in a timeless position of dissatisfaction. The adolescent's wish for certainty activates a search for an idealized love object that is both a reactivation of the depressive position and a manic attempt to resolve it (Fletcher & Benjamin, 1990). The adolescent submits to a limitless superego as a way to both protect the link to the omnipotent Other and, through refusal of ambivalence, to prevent access to the Other. Ironically, it is a position that refuses transgression, that idealizes the law.

For the adolescent, the polymorphous sexuality of childhood is truncated by a belief in the possibility of absolute satisfaction (Kristeva, 2007) via an object of desire. Adolescence marks the point at which sexual identity is idealized as unitary, where increasing school pressures to be intelligible crush more imaginative ways of presenting ourselves. A belief in a complete complementarity between the sexes marks adolescent belief in "total desire", while its inevitable unattainability shakes the adolescent psychic structure. This causes the structure to become permeable to transformation but sometimes, to disintegrate under the weight of desire and frustration.

As Herculine enters adolescence, she has a sense that her body holds a mystery for reasons that she vaguely understands. She is preoccupied with the peculiar "secret" of her body, a vague knowledge that is mixed up in a double anxiety: of being penetrated by the scrutinizing look of the Other, and of the Other's knowledge of what is missing in her body. She both fears and yearns for this Other that will solve the enigma of her body. For Herculine, the fantasy of gender complementarity, which is implicit in the convent's "girls only" policy, corresponds to the adolescent's need to believe in a phantasy of ultimate satisfaction (Kristeva, 2007) via the union of the two genders. It is precisely because the sexes cannot come together in the convent that the idealized notion of "the couple" is maintained. The "wondrous" years at the convent provide subtle homoerotic pleasures that are enjoyed as inhibitions.

The nostalgic pining for an imagined bliss, making good a loss that never took place, is also a denial of the erotic body that is always vulnerable to its desire. The passage of time, which announces the body's sexuality, also forces a gradual giving up of youth that in the memoir culminates with a medical "discovery" of gender that removes Herculine from adolescent bliss, thus crushing the imagined place of union. What appears as a wish for a complementary gender becomes a way to obliterate difference precisely because of the belief in the possibility of gender to completely fill the m/Other's lack, and thus provide wholeness for the subject.

As we read Herculine's diary, we may drift into a nostalgic reverie, sharing Herculine's pining for lost youth before the verdict of gender was delivered. The nostalgic and dramatic language, its timeless conflict-free air, draws me to identify with the character's innocent, non-gendered existence. However, the relief that he/she anticipated in finally choosing a gender is replaced by a death wish when the "deformity" is discovered. For Herculine, the shameful secret of the "incomplete" body turns into fear and desire to be caught and punished. Imagining that she has lived an unspeakable life, beyond the limits of what is possible to contain in language, Herculine ends the narrative, and as the writing stops she, now living as a man, ends her life. The rejecting mother's jouissance is indistinguishable from the absent mother. It is outside any narrative that could be attempted, rendering Herculine unable to participate in the pleasure of writing or of reconciling gender. Being declared a man seems to foreclose all possibility for survival.

Reading and writing the body

As we encounter the enigma of gender are we also "adolescent readers", affected by the memoir's ideality? As we read Herculine's memoir we may be surprised, perhaps even angry, when desire is overcome by a death wish precisely at the point that Herculine is positioned in gender; and yet, we may also wonder if our own surprise reveals a resistance based in nostalgia. It is at the place of reverie, of the mesmerizing sway of reminiscence and melancholia that I wonder whether I, the reader, have become the rejected. Is my reverie a repetition of nostalgia's idealization of innocence, which could lead to the concreteness of perversity? Is there a sort of disintegration that obscures the boundaries between reality and phantasy, time and timelessness in the act of reading?

Indeed, as readers of the memoir, as well as gendered beings, we ignore the transferential reactions that reveal our own trauma inherent in the unrepresentable excess of our bodies and the liminal time of reading. Is our idealization of lost time a way to exclude our own abject selves? Or rather, does being caught in the liminal time of the memoir make us subject to transition? Will paying attention to our own mesmerizing captivity reveal our vacant wordlessness of trauma, the place where nostalgia covers the intolerable impasse between lust and hatred, fusion and de-fusion?

The memoir's poetic language is a sinister reminder of the ease with which our adolescent minds collide with the idealism of a wish for a perfect return. This nostalgia would deliver us to a place where bodies do not matter or to a place where our body's completeness is idealized, as a way to remain on the threshold of time. Adolescence is a time marked by intense and abrupt oscillations between impulsiveness and repression, between imagination and concreteness, between signification and muteness.

When I read the two narratives, I am aware of my own desire for stability and the certainty that will bring to a resolution, a coming to peace that will prevent a falling to pieces. As we read the adolescent narratives of gender, we are confronted with our own adolescent mythology, our own tendency to cling to certainty and turn away from what feels like a strange Other within ourselves. The unintelligibility of Herculine's gender is hard to bear. It forces me to encounter my own unintelligibility: in the form of prohibition – as desire becomes a dangerous Other (equated with loss and absence) – and the enjoyment of domination – where normativity and certainty are celebrated – becomes a replacement for vulnerable searches for meaning (Gozlan, 2008). Is my need for certainty a container for my own gender instability? Thinking about my reading of Herculine's nostalgic novel, I ask: does reading the tragic narrative lead to an idealization that perversely denies my helplessness? If so, does this helplessness also characterize the experience of gender, which reverts us back to our adolescent longings?

Like Herculine's memoir, *Middlesex* is constructed as retrospective time travel: a journey that creates its past as it imagines going back in history to retrieve a slice of truth the body can hang onto in order to claim its authorship. Calliope's adolescent ego is confused by a desire to answer the Other's demands to be a girl when a surprising desire arises for the object of her phantasy, who happens to be a female, and forces Cal to confront the enigma of her body and gender.

Middlesex elaborates the relation between aesthetics and ethics when the gender of the intersex character Calliope is decided by a medical expert treated as the supposed subject of knowledge. Cal lies to the experts, mimicking what she believes they want to hear: she was never attracted to women, she likes boys, she likes being a girl. Calliope exposes the clinic's lie through a lie of her own. The idealized knowledge of the Other, embodied by Dr. Luc, the head of the gender clinic, falls apart as Calliope notices "what he called my gender identity" (Eugenides, 2002, p. 408). Through Cal's lies, Eugenides' novel opens up the possibility of creating something new, an invention that exposes the truth as myth through an act that is inherently transgressive.

After leaving the clinic and running away from its terrorizing notions of normalcy, Calliope comes to understand normalcy as a shaky structure, an idealized prohibition. Subjectivity begins, we learn, when identity breaks down, when one can enjoy one's transgressions and ceases to insist on absolute recognition. As Calliope walks in and out of the clinic, we see how the clinic itself is caught in its own myth, performed through the symptom of searching for an origin to gender identity. Cal's quest tells us how the tyranny of the material body, and of the armor of "knowledge", are all ways in which one attempts to settle the trauma of desire's unknown path and to foreclose the question of creativity and choice.

We may imagine writing as an activity that excludes the body, as a space of phantasy and play where thinking is at ease, unaware of its contradiction with the body. We see through Calliope and Herculine how writing comes to represent the possibility of transformation that is affected and effected by the body it struggles to capture. Something happens to thinking under the weight of the "truth" of the body. Is there a material quality in writing, which, like physical transitioning, drives the "writer", with a promise of satisfaction? Is transitioning a sort of writing at the level of the body that can become literary when it is wounded and ruptured by its own affect and incoherence?

The act of re-writing

As Cal and Herculine suggest, survival is always predicated on language. The texts under discussion ask us to consider the ways in which the act of reading also makes us into writers because we are forced to create a bridge within the self via the other (narrator). We are therefore creating a transitional space that disregards a starting point or an end, because the lines between us and our reading, between us and our objects become murky and unclear. The murkiness of time is captured in *Middlesex,* which refers us to the psychoanalytic idea that our beginning as subjects rests on a forgetting. As Cal narrates his story, the reader encounters an analytic tale where telling means forgetting. Like Cal, the reader is also called upon to make meaning of loss. We are pulled in by the details of the story but are also reminded of another story, that of the author/narrator casting a shadow on the story's interiority. It is here that the reader/analysand comes to realize the way in which the story depends on one's own reading. But do we have a choice in how we read if our stories come from the Other? Can we make the story of the Other an/Other story?

This question brings us back to psychoanalysis, where our narrative is opened up to another reading. As we narrate our origin we must re-narrate it through an act of reading and re-reading our own story. In analysis, the narrative is opened to its ambiguity in the same way that the reader's ambiguity is opened by the text. The reader is pulled by a need to answer the enigmatic question of embodiment but also pushed away from any stable answer and thus forced to make her own meaning. We become aware of our own discomfort with indecision, with incompleteness and with the gaps inherent in our own narrative. We are placed in middle-sex in the midst of our own sexuality, which is now confused and confusing. What do we think of Cal? Could we stabilize our anxiety by diagnosis or gender? What if we read Cal's narrative as the enigma of object relation, of the tension between self and other?

If we read Cal's text as an attempt to take hold of his own narrative and as a struggle with the narrative's hold on meaning, we can also consider reading as an act that is concerned with truth: the truth of the subject's desire. In our inability to say it all, our narrative reveals more than we mean and so, once we are confronted with our own unconscious, we are always in doubt of our reading. The reader, like Cal, is caught between opposing readings of gender when we are trying to find meaning within the narrative: do we believe Cal's incest story? What do we situate as cause: biology or culture? We want to understand it all, to avoid the ruffling effect of our sexuality.

The liability of our fictive character that teeters between both gender possibilities also opens us to the idea of the story itself as cause. We are called upon to surrender a literal meaning and listen to Cal as if to our own unconscious. We cannot explain Cal, because the moment we provide an explanation we give our authority to an Other. To explain Cal would be to exclude ourselves from the story. Cal's instability becomes a guarantee of our own stability. However, Cal's ability to hold on to instability and the reader's ability to tolerate the narrative's ambiguity subverts this necrotizing move. Cal becomes a master of his history precisely when he tells us "I was born twice" – it is here that he discloses his history as fiction and offers us an analytic reading of history as a dispossession: one cannot know.

Our capacity to listen to our characters' struggles with their enigmatic embodiment as a struggle to make meaning from history speaks to the way in which we are transformed through our reading. The capacity to tolerate enigma, anxiety and vulnerability in our own transferential reaction to the novel opens us to experience a "novel education" (Britzman, 2006). To become analytic readers of the story we allow ourselves to be duped by its literality. The act of reading, like the analytic act, involves transforming the literal into the literary. The analytic act requires risk, idealization, and de-idealization. The analytic experience is therefore an acrobatic act on a tight rope between ideality and emptiness – an attempt to orient oneself while walking on a tenuous link between what is known and what is unknown. De-idealization occurs bit by bit, through fragments of experiences that disappoint, miss and reveal the analyst as lacking. It is a position where the analyst's enigmatic response and her temporal presence makes possible the progressive internalization of the capacity to stay with desire.

Through the serial repetitiousness of the Fort/Da of our narrative, something that is lost is brought back by imagination. Our narrative is both omnipotent repetition and a commentary, an attempt to control the past but also a link with its residue to the present. The narrative both opens and inhibits desire, wrestling desire out of conscious constraints but also, in the confrontation with words, allowing the emergence of the possibility of satisfaction through its inhibition. Cal's shattered object of phantasy leaves his body with an unending desire, which in its hunger for an answer gives rise to archaic objects, infusing them with meaning. As Cal's belief in the stability of language erodes, his satisfaction is dispersed, no longer bound to an idealized lost object of the past. For the reader too, when history is opened to narrative and what is known is put into transit, something loosens up, becomes unstable and allows transitioning.

I briefly turn here to Lacan's notion of an Act (2002) to ask: can a subject survive her or his history? The Act addresses the intermediate nature of the transference, its ambiguous status between reality and phantasy. The analytic Act captures the meaning of sublimation as phantastical bridge between language and the body, a process that, as described before, is linked to Freud's notion of the death drive as an inhibition inherent in the drive, a return to a time before repression. This pulsating "return" continues throughout the Fort/Da or here-gone of analysis, a return to the enigma of our history, to the mixture of pleasure and pain and the suspense of knowledge.

The "Act" becomes a way of answering one enigma (sexuality) with another, bringing the concept of sublimation closer to the aesthetic conflict. The analyst's ability to hold on to a "transsexual" stance, one that can bear the pain of enigma and the aesthetic conflict that underlies the transference, implies that the analyst is prepared to take themselves as an unknown. In the "Act", the patient's narrative encounters the analyst's passion for work, her curiosity and her erotic investment through the analyst's desire to think.

The Lacanian notion of the Act, and Freud's notion of the death drive on which it is grounded, allow us to conceptualize sublimation not as an act of transcendence nor as a question of "a change in the aim" of the drive but rather as a process related to signification, where a transformation is brought about within the object. It is through imagination, which is inherently transgressive, that we encounter our own sense of time. The past ceases to be a monolithic whole and turns into a porous story of becoming that serves to replace lost certitude.

In her particular reading, Kristeva (1996) reminds us that Proust's novel is an example of how narratives create their own destiny. Like a dream, fictions condense inner life and social existence, embroidering one's fate. Being "in lost time" involves struggling with desire and wishing to go back in time. Proust, as he himself observes, is a child who has died many times with each separation from his mother, and in this sense, he is like our Herculine, whose existence seems contingent on the search for the lost mother, duplicated through a series of maternal figures. However, Proust's famous bite into the madeleine is also a metaphor for the way in which sense and thought are brought together as a container for the excess that becomes signified through displacement. As a representation of a remnant of memory, the cookie combines love and hate, the two aspects of the mother, both her tenderness and aloofness (Kristeva, 1996) in what is left of the archaic Other of lost time.

We can say, too, that the narrative is a bite at the heart of the phantasy that sheds and discards layers of "truth" from the body. Like Proust's famous madeleine, the sweet taste of memory is detached from its origin through the transference. It is transformed into something that "transcends" the time of the analysis as well as the time of trauma by becoming the crossroads of what is felt in the present and what was experienced in the past. It is, however, both and neither, and therefore it blurs the boundaries between love and hate. Like the faded taste of the cookie and with it the nostalgia of memory, the passion of the transference is bound to fade and the origin of pleasure is discovered within the self (Kristeva, 1996). Proust's difficulty in retrieving the experience, like the dissolution of the transference, creates an empty space where meaning breaks down and clears the way for desire to transform the taste into an image, hence to transform history. A memory is turned into literary fiction, a re-invention of origin.

If subjectivity relies both on libidinal investment and its inhibition (death drive), is there a similarity between the analytic handling of the transference and the dispassion required of a mother who needs to contain her own madness in order to allow the desire of her child to be put in transit? Kristeva (2010) offers a way of thinking of the function of interpretation as a return to the Fort/Da of identification–disidentification between the infant and its mother. In the act of interpretation, the analyst both identifies with his patient's pain/pleasure and then offers signs that create distance between things and words. I think here of the way in which interpretation sets up a sort of "fetish play" where the analyst offers words as objects of play, while continuing to share "sensations–perceptions", "as from a mother to her child" (Kristeva, 2010, p. 205). Kristeva reminds us that the analyst's words are "fetishes" of sorts, precisely because they are not concepts but rather word-objects that the patient "receives or refuses, cannibalize or defecates" (Kristeva, 2010, p. 205). In other words, psychoanalysis turns polymorphous perversion into a desire to know through the analyst's ability to identify and disidentify with the patient's perversion.

Phantom writer

I am reminded here of the meeting of the internal worlds of the analyst and patient that sets in motion infantile and adolescent phantasies, projections, introjections and identifications. In my analysis of Sam, a 17-year-old biological female who "feels like a man but wants to dress in women's clothes", I often find myself oscillating between feeling over-stimulated and dead. One such instances happens in the way in which Sam comes to a session exhilarated about "wanting to cut" her breasts, expressing an urgent demand for a letter that confirms her readiness, only to express anxiety and disappointment about the possibility that in the next moment she will change her mind. She wants to be "flat-chested, like a boy" but hates the idea of being a "man or a woman". She desires to be "both" and refers to herself as a "scene kid . . . like gothic, only different, we are androgynous – not man, not woman".

What strikes me about Sam is not her androgyneity but the refusal, the "not" that is attached to her gender. She does not expect to feel content in any embodiment and does not know what will make her happy. She says, "I want to be like Lady Gaga, glamorous, but not as a woman. I want to be a boy, but I hate facial hair and muscles". I note the passion she often expresses in images of youthful bisexuality, of Lady Gaga and the adolescent quality of the images – representations of an idealized, genderless, conflict-free existence. I also notice the inherent disappointment her ideal entails. Like the urge I feel when reading the intersex narratives, I am aware of the wish to be relieved by the stability of "truth": when will she choose her gender? I feel a wish to dispel the phantasm of the ideal, to protect the patient from disappointment. Sam looks at me for an answer: "You tell me what I want to be. I am paying you to help me decide."

I remind her that we are both grappling with something that takes time. But I also say, "you want me to decide for you". This makes Sam enraged: "Of course! I am paying you, and it's taking too long. You are wasting my money." I take note of the anal attacks, periodic urges to cut and instances of nausea following interpretations that leave her vulnerable. Sam often stares at me with a deadening look, waiting for me to stimulate her. She describes feeling excited about coming to see me, only to be disappointed as she arrives. "I have nothing to say", she declares. "You do the talking. I pay you."

I have found myself caught in a desire to provide Sam with the letter she so longs for, to endorse her request for removal of her breasts, colluding momentarily with the euphoria of limitless pleasure. "I know I'll be happy", she says; "all I want is to be a little bit of both". But over time, we both know that the urgency is followed by disappointment and a turning to the Other who will desire for her: "is that what I want?"

Sam describes her parents in idealized terms: "My mum is cool, like a friend. We talk about each other's sex life." Yet at other times she is utterly disappointed: "My mother did not come to my graduation." Indeed, in the transference I feel called by Sam's silence, to intrude and fulfill her requests for me to talk and make her decisions. I am asked to stimulate her, to satisfy her, and when I inevitably fail, she is both triumphant and sad. I feel caught between a need to please her, satisfy and enliven her, on the one hand, and feeling deadened, depleted and having an urge to repel her, on the other. This paradoxical feeling of being caught speaks to the way Sam is caught in time, a dead zone where she desires only in split moments of paradox, which are instantly turned to emptiness. This is also illustrated in the way she often feels excited to come to the session, but her excitement soon turns to boredom. In a recent session she said she felt "still happy to be here. You haven't ruined it yet". She then spoke of her fear of driving and her reliance on her mum: "[She] does not let me do anything on my own and tells me how I feel." I told Sam that I wondered if her loss of excitement once she gets to the session is a way to take space away from me, so that I will not tell her how she feels and make her feel dependent. Sam laughed, saying she'd read about transference in school. She wondered if she gets into fights with me because "it is easier than fighting my mum".

If these enactments are remnants of adolescents' storms, they are also part of an eternal question of gender that, in Sam's case, is animated by the paradox of her embodiment and her inability to enjoy this paradox. Adolescents ask: "Who am I really to you?" (Britzman, 2012, p. 16) at the same time as they try to escape the answer ("I am not this, I am that"). Can the analyst share the patient's perversity, her "need to believe" without destroying her capacity to think? In Sam's case, sharing her need to believe would mean being affected by the spell of the paradox that hovers over the session, yet not dispelling it. It is this oscillation between freedom and certainty, love and hate – that is, the axis of trauma – that brings the analyst and the patient to a point of breakdown and to a potential creation of new meaning. But the analyst is not protected against his own adolescent desire for order and perfection. I frequently find myself drained of my ability to think by the vacant look of the adolescent who has just announced, "you tell me", or "I have nothing to say". I feel grabbed by the transferential timeless passion, with a mixed desire to provide the letter and settle her anxiety and aggression but also with a need to rescue her from her proposed "mutilation".

In part, it is through my own writing that I attempt to represent the vomit, faeces and void that are parts of the emotional mess my patient and I create. My writing becomes an act of sublimation, an attempt to channel and contain my own reactions. What I am trying to convey through my writing is the importance of the analyst's ability to embody the un-signifiable chaos of the patient and hold in tension the ambivalence towards the objects that are treated by the analysand as concrete and whole. The patient's aggression, as a way to hold the object in time and the self outside of time, is linked with the passion of meaning-making. The nostalgic hold protects the analysand from aggression's ruin and prevents creativity, which depends on this ruin. In analysis, the repressed trauma underlying idealization is recuperated as a silence, a stare and the abject body. For Sam, the wish to cut off her breasts may represent the encompassing mother who, in her inaccessibility and intrusion, is internalized as a whole. In other words, does Sam's self-presentation as indecipherable reveal that she feels only too decipherable? These unanswerable questions open the analyst's mind to what is foreclosed to memory. This "amnesia", a blank space, hides the lost passion (phantasized maternal "hold") and is traced as a story-in-the-making within the analysis. Mobilizing frozen time through the analytic passion, it inhabits the paradox of the transference like a live wire. The myth, like the transference, depends on its own destruction when, through its own inquiry, it becomes subjected to its paradoxes and hence, to time.

Like Proust's retrieval of lost time through the pathos of writing, the narratives of *Middlesex* and Herculine, as of my patient, expose one's origin as a phantasy, a place that, much like analysis, is always "no longer" and "not yet", "fugitive traces cut off from past or present" (Spivak, 2010, p. 58). Through literature we have encountered two scenes of survival: the author's capacity to deal with the emotional scene that produces a character, and the character that elaborates the material to be worked through. The book tells us a story of the narrative of the body, of writing on the body and of writing a body. We are dealing with the author's social phantasy of transsexuality, which also goes against the transsexual discourse, too often caught in a phantasy of knowledge, where the story of origin often begins with certainty: "I always knew", which serves as "after education" – Nachträglichkeit – and a negation: there is no "always" for the temporal subject who keeps re-writing herself from the moment of speech.

Conceptualizing gender as a response to a "libidinal difficulty" (Pluth, 2007, p. 160) presented by psychic difference places gender closer to a symptom. Gender is a site of collapse, a deadlock, a condensation of signifiers that, through analysis, becomes a tolerable myth. As a psychic response, gender is also a container for the irreducible split that cannot be represented, only repeated as a feigned performance – a wink that enables us to survive and transform. *Middlesex* and Herculine Barbin also show us the way in which it is within our nature to go against nature and that there is no grand plan to put us in a reproductive scheme.

The dilemma psychoanalysis confronts is that the psyche is not biology but, at the same time, it is subject to the determinants of the body. The reader, like the analysand or the writer, begins in misrecognition and, often, the self goes missing. Our narratives, as well, carry a kernel of indecipherability, as our expression of loss. The truth of the body is that there is never an original body and therefore no body is ever false. Coming to terms with our own indecipherability allows us the freedom of kneading raw material into shape, which can bring unexpected coherence to experience. In analysis, we tell our story of gender and our theories of becoming that are revealed as pathos. Our re-birth is ushered by giving voice to the parts in ourselves that cannot speak and to which we can "return" through the pathos of imagination. The body as a representation cannot give expression to the unspeakable, to sexual difference, only brush against it through the way it is narrated. This means that we always read and write our bodies in the shadow of death and that temporality preserves our desire for transformation, for a renewed life.

Our narrative is always in excess of factual events, and always a creation. It cannot be recycled or recreated, only re-found through partial objects that come together – pain and pleasure, trauma and beauty – when woven and inscribed on the body like a monument. Uniting beauty and truth, phantasy and traumatic knowledge, through the fiction of a narrative that can be told to an other (no longer a subject supposed to know) is the only recourse to re-find the partial object. Like Cal, psychoanalysis tells us that while we do not control the "accident" of our history, our choice lies in how we tell our story. Cal's enigma has not settled; but Eugenides returns us to the place of missed understanding to ask: "what will happen next?" A question is opened in analysis that reminds us that our narrative is a return that contains the unknowable truth that cannot be anticipated. The unruliness of sexuality also reminds us that analysis cannot privilege meaning, as we are bound to encounter only fragments, traces and partial objects.

Chapter 4

Transsexual surgery
A novel reminder and a navel remainder

On the cover of Gherovici's *Please Select Your Gender* (2010), we see a slender figure dressed in feminine clothes standing in front of a toilet, legs slightly spread, as if ready to urinate. The woman (or man?) stands facing away from us, with hair tied up in pigtails in the fashion of little girls, and wearing high-heeled boots. Readers are pressed to articulate what they are seeing. Is this a man or a woman, a transsexual or a transvestite? We may look at the cover over and over and over, but we cannot walk away with a sure answer. What then renders this figure so indeterminant? Does the ambiguity reside in our ideas of what gender should be, or in the figure's actions? Gherovici's book cover suggests that language and the body do not get along. Knowledge, all at once, settles and destroys meanings.

Historically, the medical profession has approached the transsexual as a problematic figure who cannot accept the limits of the body, or who treats the body as a fetish, thus insisting on becoming a "real" man or woman as the means to become complete or whole. Sex reassignment surgery (SRS) is often treated in psychoanalytic literature as evidence for such a conceptualization, and surgery is seen as both a mutilation and an omnipotent attempt to enact a phantasy of rebirth in order to reach an ideal construction of another sex (Gozlan, 2008). The request for SRS is often viewed as a hysterical idealization of the Other's completeness, an urgency to settle the question of identity, and hence foreclose the uncertainty on which subjectivity depends.

The transsexual presents both an insistence on medicalization of the body and a challenge to it. As a challenge, transsexual surgery may also signify an "act" that traverses phantasy. In this view, transsexual surgery is a means to claim one's desire, altering the body for further elaboration over the course of life. Such transitions can be given meaning through the analytic endeavour. Via the transference, analysis, after all, repeats the relation with the Other where patients come to recognize themselves as incomplete and alone. Even as transsexuals rely on medicalizing their body, they must challenge this medicalization to give meaning to embodiment. The question of meaning for the transsexual will be illustrated through Freud's understanding of appearance and disappearance (Fort/Da) as a way to handle lack.

Identification and the body's excess

Paul Verhaeghe (2009) analyzes the problem of the body caught between pleasure and pain. He considers this conflict as the grounds for which the Oedipal myth was conjured. In its original help- lessness, the body of a newborn infant is subjected to its own sexual tension, both unbearable and pleasurable. Something within in the gap between ego and body cannot be grasped or represented, and this lack is projected outward to an external Other. Gender becomes a container for one's desire to close the gap, yet desire serves to keep the gap open. These imagined attempts at closing and opening, and satiating and creating, desire take many forms, although everything depends upon the psyche's ability to tolerate absence.

One way to think about opening and closing desire is to remember how Freud links hysteria to writing a novel. In 1893, Freud wrote a paper in which he established the hysterical symptom in the domain of the psyche (Freud & Breuer, 1893). He had noticed that his cases read like novels (Britzman, 2006). This led to a theory of hysteria that conceived the subject's illness as part of "a story with its own style" (Britzman, 2006, p. 19), what Britzman describes as a narrative that creates and prevents meaning. Psychic life is created by fiction – "a phantasy of knowledge" – a "motivating fiction" that keeps the subject desiring, through a search for total satisfaction. Although this is never achieved, the lack keeps the subject engaged in a search. The subject, as Britzman observes, "wants to know against all odds" (2006, p. 18).

Freud came to view the story embroidered in the analytic process as a novel that links the symptom with the patient's place of suffering. The work of analysis becomes a "theory of distance" (Britzman, 2006, p. 17). For Freud, hysteria involves two interrelated concepts: conversion and identity. In hysteria, an instinctual drive is represented by a symptom – that is, in hysteria the symptom remains close to the "effects of the unconscious" (Adams, 1996, p. 7). Hysteria is much like a dream where the symptom draws us into the vortex of the unconscious phantasy.

Whereas Freud situated hysteria as a problem of identification with both man and woman, the universality of the hysterical symptom may be more accurately expressed through Adams' (1996) framing of the hysterical dilemma: there is identification with one, and also identification with the other. We are reminded by Green (as cited in Perelberg, 2008, p. xvi) that identification, in contrast to identity, is "a mode of thinking in the unconscious", and as such is linked with the phantasy of the primal scene where masculinity and femininity oscillate and there is fluidity between positions and ideas. Identity, in contrast, is a defensive illusion of unity that is opposed to the fluidity of masculinity and femininity. It is defined in terms of one's image of one's body and conscious ideas about the self. The fluidity of identificatory processes, however, may overwhelm the hysteric, who confuses reality and phantasy (e.g. phallus and penis), and lead to a search for certainty. In the hysterical solution, feminine and masculine styles of loving are dissociated (Kristeva, 1991).

If hysteria comes close to the expression of the unconscious, the symptomatic form it may take will elaborate the struggle between the foreignness of the unconscious verses the embodied self. Estrangement comes to be expressed through gender – a mark that is applied to the object – that, like a name, is given before birth and will become a bearer of a string of meanings, and then a metaphor for difference itself. If the unconscious is something that surpasses the embodied self and is the Other, it will be "a stumbling block" (Pluth, 2007, p. 17) to the self's attempts for signification, processes that, through language, regulate what is in excess of the self's symbolic capacity.

Gherovici (2010) considers both the hysterical and the sinthomic solution to the problem of desire and its excess. Both positions are attempts to regulate jouissance. However, the hysterical stance believes in satisfaction and is involved in an endless search for a guarantor. That stance is based on a belief in the phallus. Indeed, most literature grounds transsexuality in a hysterical race toward the creation of a body that will offer complete satisfaction to the Other, or as a way to evade desire altogether by transgressing the limits of the body.

Gherovici draws on Lacan's concept of the "sinthome" (2005) – a position situated in doubt – as a way out of the certitude of pathology. In the sinthomic position, alienation with phallic signifiers is accompanied by something else – a lack, or an absence that leaves room for meaning. Signifiers may then be used autonomously, in "profound indifference to the Other" (Pluth, 2007, p. 104). However, this involves giving up the "complacent", comfortable relation to the other (Fink, 1995, p. 72) in a way that permits signifiers (e.g. of masculinity/femininity) to be used in a way that is not bound up with predetermined meaning. Transsexuality as a position in relation to jouissance can be only considered when castration is not taken literally, when the Oedipal story does not lose its phantasmic qualities, and when its psychic author remains the subject.

Transsexuality as sinthome

Lacan's captivating concept of sinthome points to a different route out of endless suffering. In contrast to the hysterical position, which takes its symptom as truth (a true filler for the Other's lack), we create a sinthome when we identify with our symptom, that is, when we no longer believe in the truth of the symptom but see it as a creative product of the self, and hence take ownership of it. We may enjoy our fantasy of the Other but doubt its authority. We suture phantasy and doubt together, willing to make do with the scar that at the same time divides and unites us. The unconscious gives shape to lack through metaphor. In the imaginary world, there is no lack. The lack is a remainder that is left at the door of the symbolic world of language, the sensations, "things" language fails to signify (Efrati & Israeli, 2007). The symptom comes to hide the lack, but it also hides desire, an aspect of demand that cannot be satisfied (Lacan defines desire as demand minus need). The sinthome expresses the coming to terms with the fact that partial happiness is possible only in the face of lack.

This is in fact the scenario proposed by Gherovici for the transsexual question. Gherovici introduces the example of Schreber and Henry (Lacan's transsexual patient) as a way to consider how the absence of a paternal function – a third space – creates a phantasy of a claustrum for which different solutions may be employed as a way out. Transsexuality may also function as a way out of a claustrum, and in this way can introduce difference but in a way that circumvents "the name of the father".

Lacan turned to the Schreber case when treating a transsexual patient named Henry. He argued that the madness of the father's discourse in the Shreber case could not function as a representation of the law but instead "was" the law. The law and the real became one. Similarly, in Henry's case, the paternal function had failed, leading his patient to confuse the phallus with the penis. The penis could not be symbolized, making his whole body feel like "a foreign body" (Gherovici, 2010, p. 14). Gherovici posits that Henry's demand for surgery illustrated the way in which sexual difference needs to be embodied in both the symbolic and the imaginary realm. For Henry, it was the deferred wish for surgery rather than its granting that protected against the Other's jouissance. The surgery (which he never underwent and never fully pursued) represented a subtraction of a "privileged piece of flesh from the Other's jouissance" (Gherovici, 2010, p. 159).

In Gherovici's account, the surgery has a relational quality and paradoxically becomes a way to peel off the crust of signifiers that enclose the real body, and so "carve out" a lack. Gherovici demonstrates how unconscious sexual positioning does not depend on the literal organ or on a performative identification with an image. Within the unconscious, the proclamation "I am a man" or "I am a woman" exemplifies the inherent alienation in subjectivity that is derived from the very fact of language. We are split on the choice of "meaning" – that is, the signifier that comes from the Other or "being" – of the subject (Gherovici, 2010, p. 197). This impossible position, Gherovici argues, is a terrific conflict, one in which choosing meaning comes at the cost of disappearance under the Other's signifiers, while choosing "being" risks losing meaning, which comes from the Other.

In Lacan's theory of anxiety, jouissance is a resistance to symbolization that in phantasy is made into something the Other wants (Pluth, 2007). Through fantasy, the subject makes himself or herself what the Other may enjoy. This also places the subject at an impasse because of the impossibility of jouissance: "Something of jouissance continues to escape the phantasmatic situation of jouissance" (Pluth, 2007, p. 87). Anxiety is twofold: of being the object of the Other's desire, and of being expelled from the Other as a failed object. In both situations, the subject's status in relation to the Other is put into question, so jouissance can be phantasized as an encounter with death (Pluth, 2007). It is the anxiety of falling into the phantasmic hole that touches the reality of the lack of the Other: the uncovered gap between the subject and his or her Otherness.

Lacan distinguishes between strategies to handle anxiety over the jouissance of the Other. One is through acting out, which may be akin to the hysterical solution of addressing the Other directly and believing in a possible reunion, "if only . . ."

A second is what Gherovici attributed to some forms of transsexuality that create a sinthome, which she views as consistent with Lacan's "passage to act" (and Pluth attributes to Lacan's third strategy – an Act). Gherovici interprets the "passage to Act" not as a direct message to the Other, not "a message addressed to anyone, but rather as implying a disintegration of the subject who, for a moment, becomes a pure object, a leftover signification" (Gherovici, 2010, p. 203).

In a clinical example of a bulimic patient, Gherovici argues that, in the act of throwing up, her patient Linda was "swallowed by jouissance beyond castration" (Gherovici, 2010, p. 206). Eating and vomiting were a way in which Linda held onto jouissance to ensure her rejection from her mother. In an ironic way, it was her way of carving out a lack in the Other as a desperate attempt to feel desired by the Other, as her maternal discourse did not have room for "the name of the father". We learn that, in her analysis with Gherovici, Linda was able to take control of her symptom. She no longer saw the Other's desire as a demand for her to embody "the primal cause of this desire". We learn that Linda became a culinary artist and that food became the medium through which the remainder of jouissance was "cut away from the body" (Gherovici, 2010, p. 208) and made open to interpretation, a surface that could be written upon.

Similarly, Gherovici posits that, in some instances, a transsexual body is a self-created fiction that allows a subject to live. She particularly focuses on the transsexual's drive to write, which she studies in numerous memoirs of transitioning, as well as in the process of transitioning itself. Both entail a particular narrative that becomes a story of origin, such as is required by health authorities as a prerequisite for the initiation of hormone treatment. For Gherovici, this process of writing is a transformative rewriting of a story of origin that inscribes difference. It involves a reinterpretation of the subject's stance in relation to the Other. Finally, the process puts subjects in the role of authors of their own destiny.

Indeed, transitioning can be conceptualized in this way as a rebirthing of oneself; however, this rebirthing is not only in a sense imaginary or real, but also holds threads of the real, symbolic and imaginary. The new narrative holds the possibility of changing the structure of the subject in that the Other no longer plays an important part in it, and this very gap between the self and the Other is mourned. It is a transition that accepts failure as inevitable and is willing to live creatively with the "between zone", as if in the place of a "suture" created by bridging the phantasy of complementarity or satisfaction, and the lack, joining meaning and meaninglessness.

In the transsexual sinthomatic position, the body and its narrative are held together by "sutures", whose visible scars reveal its precarious composition. The "lost object" is recovered through writing but is not believed. It merely functions as a placeholder for desire (Gozlan, 2008). Signification and endless pleasure, language and sexuality, can be as if "sutured" together and contained by what Lacan calls an "Act" – a transgressive move away from complete identification with the Other's desire, to identification with lack (2002). An "Act" does not describe movement or a physical action. It refers to a signifying act that captures both certainty and doubt. It allows for desire but anchors it in a fleeting imaginary, an "as if". It is both concrete and symbolic – a "thing" (e.g. a body) and its representation that does not completely let go of the unreachable and unintelligible kernel. I argue that, within the Lacanian framework, transsexuality can function as this "Act", a way by which the subject inscribes difference to bridge the gap between lack and satisfaction, where the phantasy of the body's imagined "wholeness" (its imaginary unity through gender) is linked with absence of the Other (e.g. there is no preordained meaning to femininity or masculinity), "a realization that there is no Other of the Other, as it were, acting as a ground" (Pluth, 2007, p. 148).

Identification with the act: a clinical fragment

If the symptom is a way to fictively hide the basic truth of lack, the purpose of the analytic act is to come to terms with lack by creating a narrative, embroidering a personal myth where enjoyment is shaped by a plot that is written by the subject rather than by a phantasy that is believed in. Each symptom contains a hidden wish, a sinthomatic solution or "act", and hence the analytic act functions as a way to turn this wish from a complaint into desire, keeping the subject in movement.

Can transsexuality, we may ask, which involves corporal intervention, be considered sinthomatic? If gender is a way to symbolize sexual difference within the self, a sinthomatic creation of Otherness through one's own jouissance, this difference does not lie exclusively in the body or in conscious identity. For Gherovici, the sinthome is where surgery and writing intersect. Transsexual writing is a way in which transsexual subjects embody "sexual difference" by rewriting a story of origin that invents them, and thus releases the phantasized hold of the Other's determinations. This rewriting, in literal form and as a historical account of one's becoming, is a way in which the paradoxical concreteness that Gherovici observes in some transsexual desire to close the gap between the body and its lack becomes loosened.

I illustrate transsexual desire with a clinical fragment of one of my patients, whom I will call Aron. His early recollection may be analyzed as a means of elaborating the move from hysterical solution to traversal of phantasy. Aron is a female-to-male patient in his late 30s who recalls at the age of three being held by his father but feeling uncomfortable (as if he was suffocating or absent). He recalls crying and wanting to be handed back to his mother, but then finding this intolerable and crying again, wanting to shift back to his father. This switching from mother to father, father to mother, occurred several times, accompanied by uncontained anxiety, anger and feelings of being suffocated by both parents.

Aron's depiction of his parents portrayed an extremely self-absorbed pair. He described his mother as a passive martyr who turned her attention and investment to her husband at the expense of her children, and portrayed his father as a volatile man, sadistic and envious of him. Aron felt that both parents were actively invested in stifling his attempts to separate by restricting his exposure to outside circles (e.g. not allowing him to go to friends' houses or invite friends round) and becoming overly dependent on him. Aron's early recollection of moving from one parent to the other, unlike the Fort/Da game, was directed at his parents and was infused with a wish to receive the containment he craved for. Perhaps it also held a grain of what would become his ongoing struggle to dis-identify with them both.

Aron wondered whether his own transsexuality might have functioned to avoid him becoming engulfed by his parents, perhaps being a way to free himself from the claustrum of their projections. He felt that his new genitals were "finite", "symbolic" representations of organs, that were "functionless and cannot reproduce", a cut into a phantasy of "generational transmission". He described his new genitals as "a closure of a cavity and at the same time useless organs, leading nowhere". I had an image of a navel: a useless organ, a cavity, finite, leading somewhere and nowhere. Yet Aron expressed feeling good enough about his new penis, stating that analysis had somehow allowed him to think in a novel way about gender. He came to speak of his transitioning as helping to maintain a fantasy of cohesion and as a novelty, the beginning of a process to embody masculinity, however tenuous this work might be.

I told Aron of my association with the concept of the navel as he spoke of novelty. He associated to the scars on his body following surgery and how they marked "a closure to continuity", by which he meant "organs that cannot procreate or connect". Aron felt that he had "disconnected" a link to his parents that threatened his ability to separate and become his own person. He also felt that he had somehow linked phantasy to reality in the analytic process in that he no longer believed in the possibility of cohesive or complete embodiment (e.g. becoming a "real" man), yet he created a comfortable coherence for himself through a semblance of psychic "procedures" that began after his surgery, once he was forced to contend with his scars. For Aron, surgery may have begun as a phantasized release from the Other's entrapment. However, the analytic "act" became a creative way of instilling meaning in a place once saturated with the phantasy of parental authorship. He felt that, through the analysis, he was "pushed beyond [his] body", yet made his body into a better container that was able to "hold a sense of coherence".

Transsexuality may be considered as one route to inscribe difference in the same way that there is, in any creative construction, also inherent destruction that creates the external world. For Aron, surgery perhaps began as an unconscious way to close the possibility of being sucked into the Other's grip. In a phantastical sense, the transsexual body can no longer merge with the parental image. Aron was aware, at some level, of the phantasy that he could not be usurped by his parents' needs in his transsexual body. He would not be an object of desire for his parents in the sense that, at the level of phantasy, his body could no longer be reduced to the phallic desire of the Other.

SRS makes organs into symbolic "stains" in the same way that cutting the umbilical cord leaves a mark. Like a navel, an imaginary point of origin, the genitals also represent a phantasy of a lost unity. Both spaces mark an imaginary point of separation and union, linking and unlinking, creating and destroying, birth and death. Sex reassignment surgery becomes a way to rupture the imaginary link to the Other at the same time as leaving a mark (stitch) on the body that becomes a renewed way of linking two spaces that are forever marked by a gap/scar, a sort of link that is born of the impossibility of unity. Surgery then becomes an act – it traverses a phantasy of union, giving up the phantasized Other, but having to live with a scar.

For Aron, the scar is a remainder of incompleteness and the pain of integration, as if it were a primal pictographic image representing a yearning for potential cohesion. Through surgery, this fantasy was brought to an end at the same time as it created a marking on the body, in Aron's words, "like a gravestone one has to leave behind" for a new beginning. Through analysis, this final mark was also linked with a psychic reminder of responsibility. The scar is a carving made by the self, a creation of the body that is made to "suit" a phantasy in order to make space for desire. Aron came to accept his body as "good enough" and accepted the multiple representations of masculinity that enabled him to feel "one of many sorts of men". Analysis helped Aron to move away from the literality of the body in answering the question "who am I?" and toward the ability to represent his "I" through his body.

The act of analysis is the act of becoming a subject in gender: creating desire out of a place of meaninglessness, rather than there being an incessant desire for hidden or forbidden meaning that the phantasy of castration conceals. The transsexual body can function much like free association, a technique whose aim is not to arrive at a final truth. Surgery in itself becomes irrelevant to the question of pathology, because what distinguishes an Act from an acting out is not the activity but its ability to be enjoyed as lacking. Some transsexual subjects may indeed reside in this suspended place of creativity. They may come to enjoy the incomplete body in a way that gives expression to its accidental identifications that are an inherent aspect of desire's polymorphous nature, yet they may lean on these identifications as mythical embroidery rather than as the filler for the empty container that these identifications truly are.

Transsexuality, sexual difference and novel beginning

The body moves from being a biological entity determined by an originary point to a body that incurs its history through a re-creation that comes to terms with the instability of its own archive. In this way, the surgery may signify a rebirth that resists an origin. It is a birthing of the self, of sorts, which is not tied to the phantasy of reproduction. The desire for "new genitals" does not lie in the aim of achieving unity via procreation or continuity through lineage; rather, metaphorically, it may be imagined as creating a point of origin that is closer to the navel – the scar that signifies separation from the mother, a hole that hints at an endless unknown, but is also a sign of a wounding impossibility.

Transitioning is not simply the act of surgery itself, but is also the narration that accompanies one's becoming, the acceptance of the scar that reveals separation and mending of the memory of the body. The repetition is turned, symbolically, to a place on the body that is lacking and requires signification. In a sense, the space between the body and its narration is reminiscent of a dialogue between art and writing, where the two elements function as one entity without collapsing into each other. Post-surgery scars symbolize primal components of pain and wounding, what the untrammelled image hides. The narrative and the surgery both hide a slippery link between origin and meaning that cannot be captured. Transitioning becomes a creative project that gains meaning retroactively as an attempt to recreate or repeat a preconscious (pre-difference) primary phantasized origin, an event that cannot be symbolized but appears to yearn for meaning.

Writing on the body and narrating makes the body into a centre of memory that carries inscriptions of separation and, as such, the formation of a sense of an "I". We may imagine the transsexual body as a "creation", and the genitals, much like the navel, as symbolic markers of separation and union, functionless organs that cannot link, as if the subject's sense of loss is inscribed upon them. Indeed, the meaning of the body for some transsexuals is uprooted from its imaginary essentialist qualities, yet it becomes attached to the image of the body that, like a peel, holds meaning through its endless links to the Other, although now with the realization that these links are associative and are placeholders rather than idealized truths. It is the very nature of the transsexual image, its fragility, its fear of coming apart (of being "read", "misread", exposed), that holds together the enigma of sexual difference, the controlled and stable alongside the hidden intimate, the organizing element of desire and its polymorphous nature, the riddle of sexuality and the double meaning that is inherent in every image.

Sex change involves taking a plunge into the unknown. One can never predict how the body will appear after surgery. The surgery brings the estrangement between the body and the self to the foreground. As described above, the body moves from being a historical entity determined by an originary point to a body that incurs its history through a re-creation, that comes to terms with the instability of its own archive. In this way, the surgery may signify a rebirth that resists an origin. It is a birthing of the self that is not tied to the phantasy of reproduction, whose aim is not unity via procreation or continuity through lineage. Rather, metaphorically, it may be phantasized as creating a point of origin that is closer to the navel: the scar that signifies separation from the mother, a hole that hints at an endless unknown but is also a sign of a wounding impossibility, a point of creation that is born of destruction, a cut that creates an external reality.

Like the navel, post-surgery genitals are not live organs but scar tissue, representatives of a novel way of working through impossibility. They become a reminder of impossibility and meaninglessness, a hole leading to no certain place, but they also become a novel remainder, a sort of leftover of an impossible wish, carrying the mark of the endless desire concealed in the wish. The navel is an imaginary "spot of archaic emergence" (Ettinger, 2002, p. 88) on which life depends, but it has to be closed. It is a phantasmic spot that may bring us associatively to the primal scene where incestuous cravings and their prohibition converge. Any being beyond phallic certainty requires this potential to transgress incest prohibition. Transgression and taboo coexist in the unconscious (Ettinger, 2002) and represent the way in which timelessness and meaninglessness turn into meaning that is invented symbolically. We may imagine the navel as a sinthome, a mark of a cut that makes the incestuous an impossibility, which is inscribed in every relation.

Like a scar (which links two surfaces but is also a revelation of a gap) or the navel (which is both a "hole-mark" of unity and an absence), transsexuality as sinthome involves bringing together masculinity and femininity, certainty and death, in a place of constant suspense. Through the analytic act, the point of joining/unity and absence is carried through in all relations, making them "trans-subjective", a swerving/touching/not touching relation without relating (Ettinger, 2002).

Imagining sexual difference as an act of linking that is so bound with affect, anxiety about contact or absence, swerves it away from the concreteness of the phallus, which is resurrected defensively as a protection against difference itself. Sexual difference is now changed from reference to impasse into a mystical canopy, a mystical sense or "perceptive relationship" (Fachinelli, 2007) that also creates an unconscious flame nurturing an illusion that is born of the suspense of surrender, a being that is rooted in "giving oneself to being alone with another one does not know" (Eigen, 2009, p. 27).

The subject's difference is a sinthome – an irreducible "zone" capable of holding "things coming from elsewhere", sensations beyond reach that are linked only loosely, a kind of knowledge that weaves phantasms out of web-like threads and delicate points of contact. Difference in this sense is always feminine, as it does not rely on phallic opposition between having and not having. Another path is opened that does not rely on fusion and rejection, having and not having. Rather, it is the very link between the subject and the other that weaves the two spaces together, creating this sense of mystical, irreducible space, on which a sense of being depends. If "knitting the self together" depends on narrating or writing, the Real that cannot be written will always make subjectivity a creative, never-ending process where impossibility also creates a space for invention. The transsexual body can potentially become this sort of invention that knots together primal imprints, inscriptions of joining and absence, that are at the edge of possibility (because, at the primal level, both can lead to death), that, like the artist's creation, is not symbolized or signified but is reproduced in the art itself (Ettinger, 2002). Transsexuality as sinthome empresses the impossibility of sexual rapport, and hence is an expression of difference.

We can say that what some transsexuals want is to weave a self that is close to the Real of timelessness and is alive because it is also aware of its death, a temporality that is a function of its lack. For this self to be held together, for it to be the "beauty" (Ettinger, 2002) that lies between phallic pleasure and jouissance, something has to function as protection against fragmentation, a kind of foreclosure that in the transsexual comes in the shape of surgery. However, through the analytic process, surgery is not the end but a beginning that, like the developmental beginnings of the "I", emerges from a negative (e.g. I am not this, I am that). In the passage of transitioning, there is a moment of certainty that is always in opposition to how others recognize one's gendered self. This opposition becomes a resistance to one's responsibility over one's conceptual and emotional "pictogram". There is an idea that the self is dependent on the Other's recognition and that the self can only begin there. Analysis helps to make space for a more abstract notion of the self, similar to the difference between representational and abstract painting.

Analysis cannot change one's phantasy but allows one to think about one's construction of the self in ways other than an originary moment in external reality, as well as to tolerate the incompleteness of knowledge. Surgery can become, through the analytic act, a literal knotting that is also aware of its own literality but that considers it as one enjoys art, for its beauty, not its phallic truth. Psychoanalysis dislodges saturated meanings and helps one survive moments of going beyond subjectivity, moments in which one can enjoy the phantasy of cohesion without believing it. Once the Other's position is mourned as an idealized phantasy, desire turns from an incessant search for ultimate satisfaction to something fleeting that can be enjoyed only in the moment, in a space that bridges reality and fantasy, in the tension of life and death. Aron's masculinity no longer lies in the future. His surgery no longer aims to phantastically mend a fractured point of origin where things can connect or lie in harmony, like a re-suturing of the umbilical cord. Through the analytic project, identity is realized as an instant of madness that can be enjoyed only in art.

Chapter 5

The "real" time of gender

S is a 40-year-old male-to-female transsexual, who, upon starting her transition, felt ashamed of her femininity. S hated being a man but she also hated being a woman. She perceived women as "inferior, weak, submissive and empty". S came to see me after moving to Ontario from another province to start a new position in her company, where she was employed as an electrician. She had brought her suitcase full of women's clothing, which she intended to wear after work hours, as she had done for the past ten years. Her decision to accept the transfer to Toronto involved what she described as a new hope of finally becoming what she really was, a woman. She planned to announce to her co-workers her intention to transition and to begin the process within the year. However, six months after her arrival in the "city of hope", her suitcase remained closed. She complained about being "unable to play" and feeling "encased in concrete".

S's appearance was quite masculine and there were no visible signs of her desire to be a woman. It was indeed as if her femininity was encased in the concrete that was her body. She wore plaid shirts and work boots, kept her hair short and wore square masculine glasses. When I saw S for the first time, I immediately identified her as male, despite my conscious attempts to change my perception of her as she proclaimed, "I am a woman inside". I felt captured by the masculine image she presented and experienced a mixture of irritation and anxiety over having to address her as female – irritation over what I experienced as a demand to be recognized as one thing while presenting herself as another, and anxiety over offending S, by treating her femininity as invisible, perhaps repeating her own attack against her well-hidden femininity.

S agreed to see me three times a week but refused to lie on the couch. When I asked her about the possible meanings that she associated with lying on the couch, she could not understand what I meant and her face twitched in a way that seemed to reflect a strange combination of anger, disgust and incomprehension. This twitch became a common response to most of my inquiries or interpretations, unless they were concrete and self-evident. She came to sessions "armed" with a report of the preceding day, which she delivered matter-of-factly. When I attempted to link her difficulty with "playing" in the session to her difficulty with opening her suitcase, she again responded with a grimace. She had no clue how the two could be related. I felt drained and controlled in the analysis with S by the deadening atmosphere between us, by having to be on guard when addressing her gender, and by the predictability that characterized her reporting and my restrained responses. Despite this difficult and tense atmosphere, S rarely missed her sessions and became extremely angry over any need to cancel or change the time of our sessions. The analytic space seemed to be the only one she felt she could control.

A year into the therapy, S met a male partner – who identified as "master/dominator" in online communications – and S was finally able to open her suitcase full of women's clothing. She described "playing" with these clothes in what seemed a highly prescribed and ritualistic manner. She became his "slave" and for a few hours a day would follow his orders, which included letting herself be tied and sitting with an anal plug for numerous hours. S started hormone therapy shortly after and gradually increased the time she spent presenting as female. She continued to present herself as male, however, and as she came to the session after work, it was still difficult for me to read her as a woman.

S wanted the changes to occur in her body "quickly", but she felt angry at herself over what emerged as her own resistance to the transition, for instance, in her feeling that she should not reveal her transitioning at work, or go out in public in women's clothes. I struggled but eventually succeeded at addressing her as female. However, something in me could not quite feel settled with S and I kept feeling anxious and angry during our sessions. I wondered about my continuing difficulty imagining S as a woman and if being a woman was something she herself resisted. S dismissed this idea, stating that the only thing holding her back from fully transitioning was her worry over job security.

As S's features softened, as a result of taking estrogen and starting electrolysis, she started experiencing anxiety over losing her "masculinity", which she equated with social status and safety. She expressed feeling trapped in a male's body, feeling disgusted by her penis and body hair, and yet she also felt trapped in her female body – a body that she associated with weakness, vulnerability and inferior status. She felt as if neither gender embodiment was liveable and described her masculine embodiment as "familiar, old and useless". At the same time she experienced her feminine embodiment as vacant and "lacking". She described looking at herself in the mirror and feeling "not quite the woman she imagined [herself] to be". Being a woman felt like "loss, a not-being". She thought of herself as an "unattractive, grotesque woman", and when she walked in the street, she felt that others could see her "lack," and was hyper-vigilant about anticipated attacks.

S persistently expressed a desire to continue her transition but delayed filling her prescription for hormones, missed her electrolysis appointments and continued to dress as a man. At the same time, she became highly defensive when I suggested that a part of her kept holding on to her masculine image, at least socially. S expressed a hatred of having to "choose her gender". She hated being a man and hated being a woman. Neither felt herself, although femininity seemed, to her, more in line with what she wanted: "to be attractive, to be taken care of, to be handled." However, femininity was also equated with being "vacant", "unsuccessful", "grotesque", "passive" and "vulnerable". S became angry at the world, and at me, for wanting to "pin her down", to force her to be one or the other so that she would fit into society's categories (which I had come to represent). She felt suffocated and encased by these categories, which she experienced as a "gravestone". Gender, for S, was not an aspect of her identity but a burial of desire, a deadening injunction that "stopped her dead in her tracks".

In the third year of our sessions, S continued to be tormented by a spiralling oscillation of gender identifications. But what, I wondered, propelled this oscillation? What did these categories – female, male, feminine, masculine – mean to her unconsciously and what could contain this oscillation? I felt as though my own mind was oscillating in and out the sessions with S. Was my anxiety over wanting to settle her gender problematic? Was I, in fact, attacking S's desire through my own uneasiness over her indecisiveness? What would it mean for S to "settle in gender"? What would it mean to become coherent to the Other through a recognizable gender, or to come to a place where the very conflict inherent in gender-embodiment became tolerable? Still, it was evident that S herself could not enjoy either gender and was equally tormented by this oscillation. If "femininity" and "masculinity" are containers, which made her feel "empty or full", according to S's description, what might these containers hold or fail to hold? For S these containers did not hold but "trapped and immobilized" her in sealed and known categories. S's oscillation, her inability to enjoy either gender, brought her to a place where nothing seemed fitting "enough". She could never feel satisfied. Masculinity and femininity were disparate wholes separated by an impassable gulf.

On the surface, S was being tormented by an oscillation created by a tension between her desired embodiment and an impossible ideal – the "norm" – with its oppressive qualities. She narrated her experience as one in which being a woman, her desired position, had to be discarded because it was socially unliveable. Being a man, on the other hand, was an impossible embodiment as well – one she refused to consider yet was unable to let go of. She was caught in a repetition both instilling and killing desire. This spiral kept her frozen in time. This timelessness was a place with no future, or a future mired in a return to a mythical past. It might have signified a wish to reunite her disparate parts into one, to be undivided, to not feel "lacking"; but S placed the impossibility of such unification in the "prohibiting Other", as a way to externalize a painful internal division that felt to her like an intolerable cut.

Cross identification

S's oscillation was a site of tension often experienced as psychic death. She seemed to be moving, but was standing still. Her activity was marked by a sense of circularity, as if she were drowning in a whirlpool created by her own movement. She put on feminine clothes only to take them off and replace them with masculine ones. She continued the electrolysis but stopped her hormonal treatment. She came to her sessions faithfully yet was unable to free-associate and often attacked her ability to think by reacting to interpretations with a dismissive twitch. She kept moving but was unable to be in transit, to create a transitional space – a potential space that could sustain tension without leading to a collapse. S seemed unable to tolerate the unknown and accept its irresolvability.

The analytic sessions became a dead-zone where any exchange was concretized and I often felt wooden and immobilized. As I sat in the sessions with S, I asked myself, can S ever dream a gender that could come out of its suitcase? I often found myself unable to think symbolically and became caught up in the splits of her gender oscillations, as if masculinity and femininity were two concrete objects either repelling or collapsing into one another. Perhaps transferentially cross-identified with S's fragile, abject femininity, I often felt placed in the position of a little, defenseless girl, leaving me with an urge to be active but simultaneously frustrated in the face of S's repetition and deadness. I struggled to find a transitional space in myself, to avoid the urge to reduce masculinity and femininity to their associative "known" social contents. I turned to the theories of Winnicott (1971), Verhaeghe (1999) and Kristeva (2002) in an attempt to approach the concepts of "femininity" and "masculinity" psychoanalytically, that is, as psychic positions taken in relation to a central lack or loss, rather than as gender identifications. In these theories, masculinity and femininity are thought of as attempts at representation of an internal struggle between unity and separation, identification and its excess.

Winnicott ties "doing" with masculinity and "being" with femininity, as psychic possibilities within the same person. The male element – in both biological males and females – "does" while the female element "is" (1971, p. 109). "Doing" is tied to "satisfaction seeking" while the experience of "being" – upon which the ability to play and form a transitional space depends – presupposes the experience of having been one with the breast but also on the capacity to repel the breast, for the registration of external reality depends upon the sublation of this fantasy. The experience of "being" is tied to the mother's capacity to create a transitional environment for her child, a space that allows for the child to experience the omnipotent illusion that he or she *is* one with the breast. But the "good enough" mother also provides the space for the infant to experience disillusion with the breast, that is, its existence as a separate object. According to Winnicott, the mother's failure to provide a "breast that *is*, so that the baby can *be*" could give rise in the infant to envy of the breast and an inability to tolerate lack (1971, p. 110). The mother that is either too intrusive or absent will lead the child to treat the breast, and eventually her environment, in a "doing or be done to" manner, in a desperate attempt to arrive at the desired satisfaction through "using" and "finding", through oral and anal eroticism and sadism.

Could it be, then, that S's struggle was marked by a split between the female and male aspects of herself, a split that sent her on an endless spiral of gender oscillation?

S imagined her femininity and masculinity as split: two irreconcilable and incommensurable positions, where neither of which was able to contain her desire.

Gender oscillation defended S from the passivity she equated with "being"; but through her seemingly active "doing", wasn't the activity of oscillation itself bringing her closer to the stillness, the passivity of her childhood immobilization? Was her gender oscillation, perhaps, a way to sustain a complete and undifferentiated identification with the mother's desire (becoming "everything" for the mother) while at the same time, a defense against feared engulfment by the (m)Other – by maintaining herself unrecognizable to the Other? In both cases the Other became an almighty Other, a prohibiting presence that protected her both from her untamed desire for unity and her fear related to this unity. We may wonder whether engenderment itself, as an identification with the Other's desire, was equated for S with a complete disappearance into the Other.

Movement and time in the primary

S recalled little of her childhood before the age of seven; however, she described her relation to her mother as one marked by abjection and rejection. Her descriptions revealed a twisted and confusing maternal discourse. She spent an unusual amount of time physically close to her mother, yet experienced her mother's stark absence. She recalled feeling non-existent in her mother's eyes and could not recall a single instance of being hugged or told she was loved. On the other hand, she was forced to spend inordinate amounts of time in sheer silence while in the presence of her mother and was not allowed to leave the house, under the guise of being protected from the possibility of experiencing epileptic seizures. S experienced one epileptic seizure that could not be explained medically. She was, reportedly, kept "tightly" close to her mother until the age of 12, when she left for boarding school. S described her father as a passive drunk who was also absent from her life.

The abjection and rejection that marked her childhood were also repeated in the transference, where I felt hostage to S's concrete thought and my separateness was experienced as a threat. S kept "spitting back" any interpretation that referred to her affect or that attempted to link her disjointed, non-affective reports with her psychic deadness and inhibition in "play". Instead, the analysis became a re-enactment of an unchanging, timeless scene where I became like S, prohibited to leave the space created by a confused discourse of wanting to move in time (to transition) and a hatred of movement.

S's struggle with transitioning, with movement, reflects her struggle with reality, an encounter with a space outside of herself. This was reflected in wanting to keep me under her control and in her lack of regard for time. She had difficulty arriving on time to her sessions, would often arrive too early, and would knock on the door expecting to be let in. When a patient left, she would not wait for me to let her in and just barged in. My constant efforts to set limits were met with a confused and angry look. She could not understand why she could not come to see me when she wanted to. She would only tolerate this boundary if I was in session with another patient. She reminded me that, after all, she was paying for her sessions.

Endings and beginnings did not exist for S, and her relation to time replicated her omnipotent relation to the analysis. She felt violated by any sign of difference and reacted aggressively in response, becoming intrusive, controlling, repelling. Time, as a representation of difference, was experienced by S as traumatic.

One way of thinking about S's gender oscillation is through the way in which it mirrored circular primal unconscious time, which is "anti-time" (Green, 2002, p. 121): a circular movement of return to a moment of origin, to ground zero. It is an attempt to endlessly replicate sameness, where there is no conflict and where "everything has to be actualized on the spot" (Green, 2002, p. 121) to halt progression and prevent experience. S's oscillation revealed her primary way of thinking and relating as a struggle with internal difference. She was unable to accept the analytic time as one that differed from her internal wishes, and the analysis became a site of power struggle over reality. She conflated her own superego demands ("you must not desire") with external prohibitions that she attributed to a "reality" I came to represent, by which she felt persecuted and confined. Her oscillation, refusal of interpretations and her rejection of the analytic time-frame seemed to operate in the service of a conflation of reality and phantasy, rejecting the differentiating aspects of the analytic encounter. In a typical disavowal, S knew when the analysis began and ended, yet insisted she did not.

We are reminded here of Freud's conception of wish fulfilment and primary processes as defenses against trauma and more importantly here, against pleasure, which is felt as unsettling and invasive (Freud, 1920). Did S's concreteness serve as a barrier between her and me that prevented desire, intimacy or closeness (any experience that may arouse longing, attachment, or arousal)? S's gender conflict enacted the same split that prevents elements associated with femininity and those associated with masculinity from touching. This concretization treats femininity and masculinity as undivided wholes, a conception that obliterates difference through a fantasy of complementarity. She could not occupy a position in relation to the other's lack because both masculine and feminine positions were experienced as fully antithetic and incommensurable with each other and therefore, as unable to completely fill the lack of the other.

In *Beyond the Pleasure Principle,* Freud (1920) understands the registration of time as a protection against internal stimuli, for the unconscious registration of delay is experienced as traumatic. What Freud seems to assert is that temporal immediacy is a defense against the tension-raising delay of time (Bass, 2000). For S, however, conscious time and unconscious time were conflated. Hers was a conflation that repudiated temporality – "the unified phenomenon of a future that makes present in the process of having been" (Bass, 2006, p. 64), as Alan Bass eloquently puts it – and hence identificatory markers – the anchoring points that construct temporal cohesive history by which she would become recognizable to herself and to others.

In treatment, S expressed an urgency to move from one gender category to the other and yet was frustrated by her inability to settle into a "good enough" embodiment. This repudiation of time was also observed in the analysis where her dealings with analytic time became S's way of controlling the tension created by her awareness of her dependence on me.

I asked myself whether S's gender oscillation might have played out a double act of registration and repudiation of reality. Her oscillation revealed an unconscious wish to be whole through her refusal of each gender category, but her oscillation also revealed an unconscious fantasy of a "unified" category. What did S know that she did not know? I think S knew that she could not be both a woman and a man (as positions in relation to the Other) but I believe that her gender split was a way of conforming to an ideal that she fantasized as "real" (real man / real woman). This normative "real" was her own superego demand through which she repudiated what "she knew" – the impossibility of reunion.

In analysis, S defended against her desire by rejecting any registration of difference between us, as represented by my interpretations and the time frame of the analysis. I believe that S equated the analysis with "being", which she experienced as dangerous. In relation to my interpretations, perceived as a "doing", S experienced herself as a passive and helpless recipient. For her, being helped, feeling vulnerable or experiencing the intimacy of our encounter also meant being "tied" to the suffocating desire of her mother.

In my view, what was problematic in S's gender oscillation was not the issue of choosing a gender, in the sense of presenting a coherent image of oneself as female or male. Rather, the problem was her disavowal of internal difference – between time and timelessness, union and separateness, being and doing – that manifested itself through gender and where masculinity and femininity came to represent polar opposites and already made categories, neither of which she could embody and which she tried to escape through her gender oscillation. Her inability to "be" was marked by the impossibility to settle into an identification that could tolerate its own otherness. Gender for S was not a placeholder for desire, a container that would allow her to be recognized by others while holding its inchoate aspects; rather, her maleness could not tolerate her femininity, and vice versa. Instead, she experienced each category as an encasing gravestone from which she needed to escape.

Here we may wonder again about S's incapacity to "be", to remain in psychic transit while avoiding the double risk of a frozen synthesis, on the one hand, or fragmentation, on the other. What had yet to be created, it seems, was a suspended psychic place between inner and outer realities, between passivity and activity, between being and doing.

We can imagine this psychic space as one acting like a membrane, linking disjointed aspects of the self while preventing them from collapsing into one another. As the infant struggles to come to terms with the separateness of the breast – an object that is also her creation – and to configure whole objects from partial ones, she is also embedded in the process of "internalization of the environment mother" (Bass, 2000, p. 204). The experience of material care is inherently linked to the infant's struggle with the contradiction between differentiating and de-differentiating drives, given that the experience of maternal care progressively introduces the infant to its otherness while providing a feeling of unity and a reduction of the tension of difference through its containing functions. As Bollas argues, "the 'other' is first experienced as a 'process of self-transformation' (1987, p. 14), "be it from hungry to full, cold to warm, discomforted to comfortable" (Adams, 2007, p. 65) and, therefore, this encounter with the "unthought known" (Bollas, 1987) constitutes a registration of difference *through* an experience of integration of disjointed parts of the self.

If we conceptualize the developmental journey of the infant as a process of increased tolerance toward the tension of difference – rather than a movement from subjectivity to objectivity – transitional phenomena can be thought of as experiences of being-in-suspense rather than as attempts at maintaining illusory control by guarding off difference and otherness. Understood in this way, transitional phenomena do not aim at the integration of instincts and environment. Rather, it is a space that tolerates the impossibility of integrating difference within the self that allows for creative potential through compromise formations. Because there is an inherent tendency to repudiate differentiation, however, this capacity is never achieved "once-and-for-all" (Bass, 2000, p. 271).

We can see how time and temporality become crucial aspects in the configuration of necessary boundaries, because temporal boundaries are internalized as differentiating environments. S could not tolerate the difference of time and treated the analytic hour as interminable. Tolerating the tension between conscious time and analytic time requires the development of the capacity for transitional experience that acts as a differentiating membrane where the contradiction between the two temporalities can be held. In the same manner, sexual difference can be thought of as a transitional experience, a creative place that keeps temporality and atemporality in suspense. S's failure to internalize this difference also marked her gendered experience, as she could not imagine a sexed body as a signifier for a hoped integration that simultaneously holds the impossibility of such integration as a deferred wish. For S, the wish for integration became a repetition of the past – a repetition of the asphyxiating proximity with her mother – rather than a desire, which, sublimated, could propel her toward a future. "Being", in a Winnicottian sense, can be read as this capacity to accept reality as compromise formation, never absolute and always in question. For S, however, the sexed body represented two incommensurable poles waiting to be reunited. Since this reunion was not forthcoming, S could not return to the past, could not settle in the present, and could not imagine a future.

Re-conceptualizing "femininity"

Was there something defiant, or even aggressive, in S's circular existence, or was it perhaps a mark of a persistent compliance with the phantasized maternal engulfment that did not permit her to be either a man or a woman, or to live with desiring or being desired? Here we may turn to Lacan's concept of jouissance, which refers to an experience of excessive closeness to the desire of the Other. Lacan refers to "feminine" and "masculine" ways of relating to the Other's jouissance as that which determines sexuation. This entails the subject's taking up a position in relation to the Other's lack. Much like Winnicott's idea of feminine and masculine elements that are beyond genital difference but respond to perceived actions of the Other, sexual difference for Lacan implies the recognition of the Other's difference. Sexual identification, as either male or female, is always "phallic" insofar as it attempts to fill the gap of the other. The inevitable gap between maternal desire and the child's desire brings the child to look for an answer to the question of how to fulfill the mother's lack. This is how, for Lacan, gender difference comes to be, as a way of identifying with the phallus. Understood as a marker for sexual difference, the phallus is an aspect of subjectivity (in both males and females) that can be taken either concretely or symbolically. Taken concretely, it represents the belief that one possesses "the answer" to the other's lack or that the Other has the answer to one's own lack. This belief, which relates to Winnicott's notion of "doing", produces tremendous anxiety concerning loss or excess and leads to a relentless search for a "better" answer to the lack. Taken symbolically, it becomes a way of "being" in a Winnicottian sense, and it is closer to what Lacan termed "femininity".

Femininity, for Lacan, does not represent a biological gender, but a position that goes beyond the phallic structure of "castrated"/"non-castrated". Thus, femininity is not an answer to the question of desire; rather, it is linked with the traumatic Real that cannot be signified (Verhaeghe, 1999). The feminine position does not refer to the absence of the phallus, as the phallus denotes representation. It refers, instead, to a position in relation to the Other's lack that is capable of deferring a hoped-for reunion between the self and its Ideal. It is linked with the secondary processes in that it implies the ability to accept temporality, deferral and compromise formations through which the subject can hold on to an image of cohesiveness that accepts its otherness, its non-completeness. The importance of having an image of self (as a symbolic phallus) lies in its ability to function as an anchor in the face of the excess anxiety associated with the subject's double realization that his identity is grounded in the Other's recognition and that there is no guaranteed reciprocity between the subject and the Other.

We may wonder, then, if what S refused was a feminine jouissance, an experience that is not contained by the signifiers of gender. Perhaps "femininity" or "being" had, for S, become equated with an underlying anxiety over passivity in relation to the engulfing lack, or jouissance, of the Other. Through maternal handling, what is fantasized to be feminine becomes equated with an antagonistic "unsymbolized" that evokes helplessness, submission and passivity. The failure of the maternal function to provide a transitional space makes this experience persecutory.

Hysteria, femininity and jouissance

The failure to take the phallus as symbol is what marks the hysterical stance. Hysterical stances can be seen as aggressive protections against the feminine position (where passivity and activity is conflated) and its dedifferentiation. At the same time, aggression is both an attempt to differentiate and difference itself; that is, aggression is a way to obliterate difference and conceal its own passivity. The failure to find a sexual identity that one can settle into as a transitory container – rather than as certitude of pure/complementary gender categories – also becomes a way to evade satisfaction, which is equated with maternal engulfment.

In his book *Does the Woman Exist?* Paul Verhaeghe describes the hysteric as one who "longs for the unity of paradise lost" (1999, p. 142). However, Verhaeghe warns the analyst not to take the hysteric's complaint at face value, that is, not to attempt to "supplement the lack of love by holding" (Verhaeghe, 1999, p. 142). The hysteric wants to maintain desire precisely because the end of desire yearned for in the fusion with the maternal figure also holds the danger of being swallowed whole or being reduced to the passive pacifier of the Other's desire. This yearning for unity "concerns another enjoyment" (Verhaeghe, 1999, p. 142), not simply the reduction of tension provided by the phallic answer. But what is this other enjoyment? Is it the mother's breast that the subject craves, or the mother's phallus? The child wants to bridge the gap between himself and the Other. This takes the form of a pretence – as the child presents herself as answer to the Other, as a true filler to the lack of the Other. Yet the pretence falls apart, standing as proof that the desired union is impossible (Verhaeghe, 1999). Through the repetition of this display, the child enacts his desire for union as well as the defense against it.

We can think of S's oscillation as a hysterical symptom, a mark of a split. The ego preserves its unity through splitting, as it simultaneously moves toward alienation from the Other (prohibition) and toward satisfaction. In splitting, the prohibition is rejected, but at the same time anxiety over the recognized danger of reality mounts. Taking refuge in a symptom is the subject's way to "take over" the danger and manage her feminine jouissance (Verhaeghe, 1999). S's gender oscillation can be seen in this way as a compromise formation expressing both her desire to carry out an attack on the Other – through resisting identification – and her attempt at protecting the Other from her hostility by maintaining a union with the Other's phantasized cohesion. As a hysterical stance, her gender oscillation expresses her simultaneous identification with and rejection of a prohibiting authority, creating a circular way of eliciting and evading desire. S's ambivalence went hand-in-hand with her hatred of ambivalence, which was reflected in her rejection of the uncertainty of analytic thinking. As the analyst, I became prohibiting and persecutory, as evidenced by S's complaint, "they/you don't allow me to be neither/both male/female". The simultaneous projection and rejection of prohibition denies the impossibility of a complete integration, since here the impossibility of self-sameness is explained through the badness of the object. For S, holding on to a bad, prohibiting object was preferable to having no object at all. One may wonder if this internal "gender war" became the only way for S to preserve this internal bad object, an attempt to circumvent the double threat of invasion and loss posed by the intrusive inaccessibility of her parents.

S's gender oscillation also enacted a hatred of desire through which the object of desire itself became a threat. Turned into phallic objects, masculinity turned into omnipotent control – static and intrusive – and femininity into passivity and non-existence. Knowledge became a defense against the unknown of desire, turning creative activity into passivity, and passive creativity into anxious "doing". Paradoxically, although S understood her gender oscillation as a refusal of the fixity of gender categories, she became trapped within their deadening "phallic" polarity thereby refusing her feminine jouissance.

Matricide and creativity: a question of time

S was not permitted to leave her mother's side. Separateness became equated with punishment, abandonment; but this closeness without intimacy was equally deadening, suffocating and violent. The impossibility of separating from her mother – overpresent in her inaccessibility – was also inscribed in S's relationship to language, as signifiers were experienced as univocal, concrete objects embedded in rigid but incoherent discourses. This suffocating closeness to the maternal discourse – both in body and thought – suggests that S was unable to revolt against the intrusive discourse of her mother, a revolt which, as Kristeva reminds us, grounds subjectivity and creativity (2002). In this section I look more closely at the psychoanalytic concepts of negativity, creativity and revolt to suggest a new way to conceptualize gender development.

"Being" is linked to gender insofar as "being" – existing as a subject – depends upon the ability to revolt against the maternal environment on which the infant's life depends. Taking a position in gender relates to the child's increasing awareness of the mother's separateness and, therefore, to the realization of the possibility that one's love object might be lost. This potentiality of loss, which inaugurates desire, compels the child to take a gendered psychic position – masculine or feminine – as possible ways of responding to maternal lack. According to Kristeva (2002), there is no possibility of sexual difference in the absence of such revolt, as the foundation of gender embodiment lies in the child's relation to the Other's desire.

S's experiences with a maternal environment that felt simultaneously intrusive and unavailable seem to have compromised the development of a separate self that could observe and recognize itself. For S, recognition by the other involved an inherent anxiety over being reduced to an object of satisfaction; hence, she felt either inexistent or at risk of being consumed by her mother. There did not seem to be sufficient space for revolt against this maternal environment.

Through its conflicted identifications, S resisted the ability to integrate femininity and masculinity, being and doing. This resistance also transformed the creative act into a dangerous transgression, experienced as an act of betrayal against the mother's closeness. S's concreteness acted as silent defence against separation, as she operated in a way that sealed any gap in meaning that might have allowed the experience of paradox or signifying incompleteness – a necessary experience for the emergence of creativity.

Winnicott (1971) relates creativity to the ability to live in paradox, to create a transitional space that is uncertain of itself yet tolerated without being resolved. Identity is connected with creativity as the search for a sense of selfhood is a never-ending process predicated on tolerating lack and incoherence. Tolerating the formlessness of the self, the timelessness of the unconscious and its "non-purposive" (Winnicott, 1971, p. 74) quality is necessary for the subject's ability to create itself. The idea is repeated in Kristeva, who understands the analytic process of "working through" (2002, p. 36) as an attempt to integrate the atemporal, to come to terms with what is inchoate and cannot be subsumed under the linear logic of past, present and future. For Freud too, the acceptance of atemporality, which he links both to death and the unconscious, is a necessary condition for creativity. The conditions allowing for transitional space are the same that make it possible for the psyche to exist between time and the timeless, between unconscious of memory and conscious linear temporality.

Sexual difference, like unconscious bodily memory, inscribes what cannot be symbolized (Kristeva, 2002). We may think of gender as a symbol that represents this inscription and the impossibility inherent in it. Like conscious time or lived experience, gender is akin to the way Kristeva refers to "working through" (2002, p. 36) – a processing of the timelessness of the unconscious through temporary symbols. In analysis one narrates one's self through signs, whose meanings are not fixed. In this way, we can imagine engenderment as a process of working-through that inserts death, timelessness, into life. The analytic process aims at creating a psychic place where death and life, linear time and timelessness intersect, and where what cannot be integrated, what is uncertain, is tolerated in liveable suspense. It is also a process of coming to terms with sexual difference as an irreducible excess between past and future, wish and impossibility, life and death.

On the analytic couch, death is inscribed within life as the trace of the unknown, of loss and absence. The symbol, in a way, annihilates the object in order to free the subject from the traumatic over-proximity of the object cause of desire. This erasure of the object at the core of symbolization marks difference as such, a difference that is then inscribed in the body, through the Other. We can posit that S struggled with the process of letting go of the primal object that grounds symbolization and through her oscillating gender (not man/not woman) attempted to equate the symbol with the impossible difference of gender. Gender ceased to be an empty container and became a saturated fact.

Psychoanalysis and the feminine position

Resisting the lure of staying on the trope of gender and treating femininity and masculinity as "known" objects with a priori meanings was my only way out of the whirlpool created by S's oscillation and of my own counter-oscillation: my feelings of deadness and confusion in the analysis. Through my work with S, I came to realize that the moment gender pretends to be real/actualized within the analytic encounter, we have left the analytic stance proper that should, in fact, allow us to move away from the concreteness of gender. In my sessions with S, I had to be careful to avoid splitting myself in viewing my function as trying to help S decide whether to transition or not. My concern was rather what S did in relation to her reality. Was she able to have an engagement that still allowed her to desire?

We may see the analytic process as an invitation for the patient to destroy her old objects, to move forward in time. This invitation links aggression, time and creativity and touches on the way in which these dimensions are related to the ability to "be". For S to move towards "being" meant to acquire a self that was in a constant movement between future, past and present. To "be" is to wander. This roaming of the self is inevitable because "being" requires contending with lack and uncertainty. Allowing a place for the inchoate in one's thoughts, that is, allowing the expression and representation of hatred, disgust, ambivalence and death in our life, permits the subject to live in a state of ambiguity or suspense that paradoxically also guards her against becoming prey to inchoateness, as representations place limits, invisible time and space constraints on the abyss of timelessness.

Psychoanalytic work involves retracing fantasies relating to the sado-masochistic ties with parental figures that constructed meanings felt as truth. The guilt that is enacted through sado-masochistic acts is inscribed in consciousness through identification with the prohibiting parents, and so symbolization, speech and ideals are also laced with guilt about the transgression of prohibition. Guilt and shame become markers of failure, of loss of omnipotence experienced through prohibition and the experience of unpleasure, which is projected onto an outside cause. Externalizing the death drive in this way justifies hatred of the outside and halts the exchange between internal and external realities experienced as incommensurable.

The phantasy of self-cohesion that forecloses imagination and the possibility of creating a transitional space can "admit to its fantasy" through the analytic act (Kristeva 2002, p. 180). The transference can then be read as a disavowal of femininity, the void of being, that reinstalls passivity through the phantasy that by "doing" – that is, by externalizing the conflict between conscious and unconscious – one cancels the lack of the maternal and hides a wish for fusion, which resurrects the maternal Other. It is through this coexisting with "nothingness" that dislodges meaning and decentres the ego, that one exists as a subject, unshackled from the maternal grip while also incorporating it as negativity, a gap, an uncertainty that opens the space for experience.

As an invitation to play, the transference introduces a form of timelessness – everything can happen in play. It also introduces a representation of "not-being" by treating signifiers as meanings in suspense, caught between coherence and the inchoate. Questioning invites the patient to re-create herself in the shadow of impossibility and of her resistance to being. S told a story of incoherence that hid a theory of coherence – not a man, not a woman, a negation of two known certainties. What is rejected in this totalizing narrative is the uncertainty behind phantasies of masculinity and femininity. Psychoanalysis introduces a fiction that rests on difference, the instability of reality, of the ego and its irrationality, of its wounding affects (De Certeau, 1988). The analytic narrative is wounded by its own affect, its own otherness, its own inchoateness. In analysis, femininity and masculinity become signifiers resting on ever-shifting ground, a flood of associations with varying meanings, infinite questions, where difference is inscribed within the very uncertainty of the terms.

As a psychic position, femininity allows us to treat objects as fictional insofar as objects do not coincide with their representations. In this sense, femininity opens up symbolization in absence through a "killing of the object", an act that entails abjection and hate (Winnicott, 1971). Without repulsion, an invitation to aggression, there will be no questioning, no sense of revolt or freedom (Kristeva, 2002, p. 226). If femininity is equated with the bottomless container of the maternal and, as such, phantasized as the abyss on the edge of which existence rests and is, it can also become a frightening, all-consuming force of dedifferentiation. S's refusal to "kill" the tie to her mother involved a terror of finding out that the mother, as an omnipotent whole, was already dead. Being depends on this "killing" of the Other – a de-idealization – which leaves a gap, a question, a porous identity, where sexual difference, fantasy and reality, time and timelessness are "traversed". Once the Other dies as an ideal, no final meaning can be bestowed by the Other. It is through this gesture that conscious identity is put to death, not in a sense of futility or staleness but in a way that enables life. The result is an ability to "be" that is in close connection with the positions of observer or creator and that can tolerate suspense without defensive activity. In this sense, analysis can be thought of as a movement from mourning to freedom.

The maternal has to be lost to be regained in a different form – not as a primordial Other but as "unreality" (Kristeva, 2002, p. 169), where the materiality of the world is "placed within parentheses" so that it can be played with as an uncertain object to be examined and challenged. In other words, certitude is replaced with mourning for the lack that allows for the object to become malleable. The body presents a contradiction: its seeming stability, materiality and tangibility seduces the subject into forgetting that such cohesiveness is a work of fantasy, and that such representations, when deliteralized, allow the subject to find again his body as lacking, hence, as desiring.

The work of analysis involves leaving "objects" – the notion of substantial ideas – behind and through free association, diverting the focus from conscious presence to absence (Verhaeghe, 1999, p. 112). Analytic readings open the door to "infinite questioning" (Kristeva, 2002, p. 147) but in this sense, they also introduce a cut by refusing to stabilize reality with an answer. In this regard, psychoanalysis is a work of letting meanings go and inviting the subject to come to terms with non-loss – since one cannot lose what one has never had. It is also a move towards freedom, where totalizing narratives become uprooted from their saturated soil and imagined as malleable. It provides a safe space where the gaps within representations are explored – unnameable gaps, which can only be offered to the Other: the analyst – in a transferential way. It is this Other with which the subject is entangled, an Other that is both inside and outside of the subject, an Other that the subject runs both toward and away from.

Analysis depends on its failure to cure just as identity can be enjoyed only in transition, as a finite yet interminable becoming shaped by desire. When identity is turned into a question, the stillness of time is opened to the infinite time of memory. We are now left with a question: can psychoanalysis dream gender outside of its concrete encasement?

Chapter 6

Re-writing the screen

> *Long you must suffer, not knowing what, until suddenly,*
> *from a piece of fruit hatefully bitten, the taste of the*
> *suffering enters you.*
> *And then you already almost love what you've savoured.*
> *No one will talk it out of you again.*
>
> From "Long you must suffer",
> Rainer Maria Rilke

Through this book, I have considered gender as a transitional space, as symptom and as defense against transitionality. These considerations situate gender as a phantasy object that mediates between the drives and social reality, that is, as a construction that links, through phantasy, subject and object. The fiction of coherence that gender provides us with constitutes a source of certainty that defends against the traumatic real of sexuality. While our gender identity helps structure our desire, it also attempts to pin down the polymorphous nature of the drive.

By now we have come to see how that which confronts us with the enigma of gender unsettles us but can also mobilize transformation. Otherness is constitutive of the subject, since the subject is always displaced by his or her sexuality, but this very displacement is what allows for the possibility of psychic development. The very concepts necessary for thinking require shattering; the very idea of difference depends on its resistance. We have come to wonder about the way in which the infantile collapse of gender and genitalia, which leans on idealization, is ruptured through the aesthetic experience through objects of art that address us but do not tell us what they mean, thus compelling us to engage in a practice of interpretation. Likewise, I have argued that the fantasy object of gender, like dream formations, require interpretation, a process through which gender is opened to its fantasy.

In the second chapter we saw how the enigma of gender can be thought through art objects whose erotic insinuations confront us with the mysteries of gendered embodiment. While these objects are genderless, at the same time they embody fantasies of gender that resonate with their own phantasized histories or origin. Similar to the effect that the enigmatic art object has on the viewer, the transsexual body unsettles the viewer's very concept of gender as known, recognizable and whole. As we get closer to an enigmatic object we experience the need to make meaning, to "figure it out", but the object remains opaque and inexhaustible, and its meaning, incomplete and fractured. The transsexual body, I have argued, opens the certainty of gender to its enigma and confronts us with the riddle of sexuation by breaking the symbolic equation between sex and gender.

We are now positioning gender and sexual difference in a curious place, on the side of phantasy and imagination. While the real of sexual difference remains forever inaccessible, its articulation through the phantasy-framework of gender materializes the regime of sexual difference that defines our symbolic universe, the very regime on which our subjectivity depends for its formation. What does it mean to claim that sexual difference is experienced in and through phantasy? Such a claim treats phantasy as the interface between inward and outward reality, as a symbolic construction (Nusselder, 2013, p. 2) that configures how we enjoy and suffer, signify intersubjective relations, and defend ourselves from the traumatic force of the real. Phantasy is that which regulates the gender scripts we embody, the ways in which we read and decipher other bodies and our own, the meanings we attach to the signifiers of gender as arbitrary, contingent and relative translations of the real of sexual difference. In short, thinking sexual difference in this way means dislodging gender from its assumed essential core in order to imagine it as a tenuous and fragile link between inner reality and social world.

In this final chapter I consider the question of what kind of conceptual shift is required to open the notion of gender, to destabilize its seemingly intelligible and matter of fact meaning. If gender is a surface onto which we project our anxieties over the enigmatic nature of sexuality, the question arises as to how we can avoid the defensive concretizations implicit in the binary understanding of sexual difference. Like Kapoor's creations, whose transitionality depends on a creation of emptiness (Bhabha, 2011, p. 188) and whose conception of "surface-as-substance" (Hardaker, 2012) and play with motion and stasis produce instability and ambiguity in the viewer, gender too must usher a conceptual collapse that will expose its veiled void. In this chapter, I consider such conceptual collapse as a precondition for psychic transformation and posit that transsexuality, when considered as a question of ethics and aesthetics, may allow us to access the anxiety inherent in conceptual instability. In other words, in considering gender as fundamentally mediated by fantasy, we face a loss of intelligibility that becomes the very condition of possibility for the emergence of a radical kind of hope, precisely at the point of loss of meaning where "nothing" seems to happen.

Absence and temporality

In studying the sculptures of Anish Kapoor, Homi Bhabha reflects on the artist's relationship to materiality and temporality. Kapoor's art, according to Bhabha, turns material into a "living tissue" (2011, p. 185), predicated upon absence. The art pieces hint at a non-substantial presence below, behind and beyond the material. There is a "non-physical thing" that is "out of sight" (Bhabha, 2011, p. 185) that is integral to the piece and that gives the material its transitory character, turning the object into an intermediate space through which something immaterial passes through. Through this "making of emptiness", the body of the sculpture's gaps and absences opens the object to its own temporality. The transitional character of Kapoor's art, according to Bhabha, resides in the experience of the piece as an object-in-process, as an object, that is, that keeps being made and re-made by the observer. In "the ceremony of passing through to something else", Kapoor's sculptures reveal themselves as contingent and relational objects, unfolding in time, like breathing, desiring beings.

Through Kapoor's pieces, then, Bhabha invokes a question about the relationship between materiality and what is in excess of it, a question that can be applied to gender's relation to sexuality. I suggest here that gender functions as a materiality that makes sexuality possible. If we consider gender as a medium that gives form to sexuality, we must also consider gender as a resistance to sexuality's timeless and effervescent quality. What would it mean to consider gender as an object that insists on representation and yet resists, like Kapoor's art objects, both the "physical and transcendental"? How can gender be opened as an engendering, transitional, malleable object?

While gender often provides us with an imaginary stability, gender identity is always out of balance, always contending with a void and, therefore, always on the way to completion, on the way to having or being "it". But the inherent incompleteness of gender (of never fully having or being "it") discloses its transitionality: we can be "it" or have "it" only in transit. The phantasized wholeness that gender offers us can only be captured momentarily in its fleeting substantiality since gender, not unlike Kapoor's pieces, "holds together those diverse spatial elements and disjunctive temporal qualities that are involved in the temporal movement of the work – that continuous play" (Bhabha, 2011, p. 186). Here we can imagine gender the way Bhabha conceives of Kapoor's pieces, as a "gathering place", both "perceptual and conceptual", caught between the temporality of the unconscious and of the imagination.

Bhabha reflects on the loss of intelligibility as a point of origin in Kapoor's art. For Bhabha it is the void in Kapoor's work, which acts as a link that "staples the flesh to bone" (2011, p. 189). In Kapoor's work, the void is a transitional space that is linked with time. It is a "space of becoming" (Bhabha, 2011, p. 189) where one can "look again for the very first moment of creativity, where everything is possible and nothing has actually happened" (Kapoor as cited in Bhabha, 2011, p. 189). Temporality is linked with the myth of origin in Kapoor's work since the making of absence through the shaping of the material constitutes an effect of difference. Kapoor's work signifies delay and repetition. His monumental pieces produce uncertainty, ambiguity and undecidability in the observer as they resist being viewed as whole and force the audience to try to piece them together, to re-member their fragmented perceptions. We are unable to locate the work's origin, its kernel of meaning, for the "first moment" of looking does not correspond to an actual starting point where an original wholeness could be grasped, but rather to a moment of separatedness. Instead, the work's "lagged temporalities" (Bhabha, 2011, p. 192), its transitional qualities, create a back and forth movement between presence and absence, time and timelessness, compelling us to look again and again, to remain in the process of signification. Bhabha links this time feature of art, its inherent delay, to the temporality of belief. Both the process of making sense of art and the experience of belief involve a return to a possibility of recreation not through objectification (e.g. seeing is believing) but through holding a transitional experience of doubt that suspends certainty and allows for hope, understood not as a promise of a return to origin but as a "leap of faith" that creates retroactively a point of origin inseparable from one's understanding in the present. Art, Bhabha suggests, like belief, stands in suspense of an origin.

Gender too is aligned with cause and creation. As the word "engenderment" suggests in its double meaning of "bringing into existence" and "coming to gender", gender is deeply tied with the subject's fantasy of origin. Perhaps gender is an artifact or invention, an embodiment of phantasies of origin weaved in our narratives of sexuation and desire. The process of engenderment, like the signifying encounter with the enigmatic art object, entails an act of incorporation and identification with a dislocated fragment, that is neither external nor internal to the self; that is felt to emanate from our core, yet places doubt at the very centre of our being. I want to suggest that gender is an enigma that rests on a belief. It too is suspended of origin, enjoyed in excess and born of doubt. As an object of desire, gender has no direct relation to true or real object, but is always made present by a "screen of phantasy" (Nusselder, 2013, p. 62). The concern with the "truth" of gender, reveals the uncertainty at its core.

Ground zero

If we conceptualize gender as a fantasy screen, artifact or belief that functions as a cover-up for the uncertainty of sexuality, veering away from the concreteness of gender also means rattling the axis of the imaginary, letting loose of the coordinates by which we are settled into subjecthood. It also means unsettling the cultural and institutional structures that support this phantasy. By conceptualizing gender a screen phantasy, the question "am I a man or a woman" is no longer straightforward; it becomes a question of ethics and aesthetics, a question of how to live. How do we reconcile the seeming permanence of identity with the transience of desire? If gender is the answer to the unstable question of sexuality, how do we dwell between a question and an answer? How do we "live" our drive? Or in other words, how do we signify our desire in light of its unpredictability? How do we maintain our belief – or intelligibility – in the face of the conceptual collapse we are inviting?

It is indeed a conceptual collapse, a loss of meaning and intelligibility that Jonathan Lear proposes as the grounds for "radical hope", the ability to survive in the face of devastation. But a transformative, "radical" kind of hope, that maintains the survival of the subject, Lear insists, can only occur at the moment where "nothing happens", at the point where time is felt to stand still, where the very essence of what counts as "happening" is lost. Lear's text, *Radical Hope* (2006), presents a psychoanalytic insight into the way in which Plenty Coups, the Chief of the Crow Nation, survives the devastation following the erection of laws that would completely change the Crow's way of life. Through his analysis of Plenty Coups' narrative, Lear weaves the concept of hope to rupture, fissure and discontinuity and situates the experience enigma at the core of loss and hope.

Plenty Coups' articulation of his tribe's experience of devastation is quite peculiar. Following the disappearance of the buffalo, the ritual of counting coups, around which the tribe's conception of success, courage and even food preparation was defined, Plenty Coups tells us "nothing happened". The disappearance of the buffalo followed the Crow tribe's restriction to the reservations, which brought with it the sudden and catastrophic end to their way of life. The coup is a stick with which the courageous warrior defended the tribe's territory. By placing the coup-stick on the ground, the warrior would state his ardent intention to fight till death if the boundary marked by the stick is crossed. In battle, touching the armed enemy with the coup-stick before otherwise harming him was considered an act of great courage, one in which the enemy was made to recognize his defeat, to recognize the Crow warrior as a victor before being stricken down. At the end of the war the coups were counted and the stories of bravery recounted; this is the ritual known as "counting coups", which, as Lear states, symbolizes "the establishment of a boundary recognized by both sides" (2006, p. 19). The coup stick was important to the tribe's survival not only as a marker of boundaries but also as a signifier by which the tribe would make itself self-intelligible. It provided meaning to tribal life, to all activities, from food preparation to the definition of courage, to what counts as "happening". Lear suggests that Plenty Coups' peculiar utterance "nothing happens" speaks to the total loss of cultural self-intelligibility that followed from the radical change to the tribe's way of life. When the tribe loses the concepts on which its discourse is based, it is faced with an empty container. The time when the "buffalo disappeared", the time of the reservation was no time at all: events had ceased to happen.

Plenty Coups' stance, Lear suggests, may call for a psychological interpretation. We may conclude, for example, that he was depressed. Lear, however, cautions us against a hasty interpretation based on an assumption that "fits the principle of humanity" (p. 4) and instead invites us to consider the specificity of "Plenty Coups' humanity". He points to Plenty Coups' vitality and activism in the years following the disappearance of the Buffalo. Plenty Coups, Lear claims, did not act as a depressed person. Instead, he asks us to ponder on Plenty Coups' enigmatic words, "nothing happened" to suggest that they call for interpretation. If Plenty Coups is referring to "happenings coming to an end" (Lear, 2006, p. 4), what insight does he offer us in regards to the "structure of temporalities"? (Lear, 2006, p. 5).

Plenty Coups' peculiar articulation of the devastation of the Crow tribe's way of life, as Lear observes, suggest something other than coming to terms with the reality principle, that is, with the impossibility of bringing back the lost buffalo. It suggests that psychic survival entails a return to a new point of origin, to a new temporality structured retroactively through a return to the point where "nothing happens". Only at the point that nothing happens, can we call our own desire into question. In what way, we may ask, is Plenty Coups' allegory useful to our thinking about gender? Situating the loss of concepts such as gender alongside the loss of a way of life of the Crow tribe may seem peculiar, for how can we compare the contingent devastation of a way of life brought up by colonialism to the necessary and desirable losses that make us move into less debilitating understandings of difference, heterogeneity, non mastery?

Here we may also ask, what is the relationship between contingency and structure in relation to loss, and how is this relationship related to the project of this book?

I would like to suggest that the allegory of Plenty Coups helps us elaborate a link between the structural losses that constitute the subject in relation to others and the contingent losses that destroys the notion of the self and other. The contingent losses experienced by the Crow tribe, its loss of a culturally articulated way of life and, correspondingly, its loss of what could be counted as happening, has the potential to destroy the possibilities that the structural losses open – the coming to terms with difference that structural losses move us to symbolize. What was lost when the buffalo disappeared was the structure of intelligibility around which the Crow tribe's way of life was articulated and apprehended and insisted upon by the ritual of counting coups. Through Plenty Coups' narration of the cultural devastation experienced by the Crow Nation, we learn how some contingent losses can destroy the conceptual apparatus upon which our very ground of intelligibility is based; where the kind of reasoning, the point of view used to make sense of something, is no longer available.

In *Radical Hope,* Lear raises two crucial questions: how can we narrate a story of cultural devastation ethically as opposed to judgmentally, omnipotently; and how can we conceive of such a story as an ethical opportunity to ask "how we ought to live with this possibility of collapse" (Lear, 2006, p. 9)? The story of the Crow Nation tells us that in the face of cultural devastation, when we can no longer rely on familiar paradigms and culturally embedded forms of insistence, people have to rely on enigmatic signifiers in order "to anticipate a future [one does] not know yet how to think about" (Lear, 2006, p. 78). Following Lear's interpretation of how the Crow Nation grappled with the question of ethics after disaster, I would like to suggest a reading of gender that breaks the confines of its intelligibility under the assumption that to conceive of gender outside of the traditional antinomy male/female constitutes indeed an experience of cultural devastation.

Fantasmatic art of disappearance

Plenty Coups' narrative poses the question of how to live with the possibility of collapse. It is a question that can also be asked as we encounter the fragility of our gender imaginary through the concept of transsexuality. Transsexuality threatens our regime of gender identities because it unsettles the gender certitude attached to biology and, therefore, the anatomical differences between "boy" and "girl" can no longer be taken as clear, straightforward signifiers. As a concept that fractures cultural meanings of gender and forces a re-conceptualization of the terms of its intelligibility, transsexuality poses a question: how to make sense of the paradoxes and discontinuities of gender?

Much like "the end of happenings" (Lear, 2006, p. 2) ushered by the disappearance of the buffalo to the Crow tribe, I would like to suggest that transsexuality holds the potential to turn our concept of gender into an enigma and to produce a collapse of the point of view through which we make sense of sexual difference. Coming to terms with the enigmatic nature of transsexuality can make us feel as if "nothing happens" because a way of life where the "truth" of one's gender is guaranteed by anatomical difference is lost. It can feel as if time stands still because what is lost is the certainty of a frame, our phantasized intelligibility.

If a psychoanalytic reading of transsexuality – one able to sustain the dilemma that the unconscious presents to knowledge and certainty – makes identity unintelligible, what would count as masculine or feminine? How can we produce a conceptual devastation to our imaginary of gender through the notion of transsexuality? Perhaps here we need to be reminded again of the peculiar link between gender and art that I have been articulating throughout this book. When we approach gender through an aesthetic framework, we treat it as an empty signifier tied to imagination, not intelligibility.

The fantasy of intelligibility inherent in gender unites "lagged temporalities", disparate spaces of time, inside and outside, being and not-being. It is also a brittle concept that is subject to devastation because the cultural universe we inhabit is fragile, arbitrary and lacking. Approaching gender from an aesthetic perspective is a way to usher a necessary collapse of our gender categories because our bodies, like art objects, constitute a materialization of an impulse toward signification while at the same time they actualize a resistance to signifiers, thus holding the potential to rupture the confines of language, to let us brush against what lies in excess and in deficit of language.

Indeed, throughout this book, we are called to transition our own conception of gender and of transsexuality, to consider gender as a transitional object and as an object in transit. Gender is an object in transit because its intelligibility relies on a symbolic construction mediated by fantasy and, as such, it is tied to sexual desire as a drive toward an experience of satisfaction mired in the endless search for the always already lost, unattainable unconscious object. As a concept that brings to light the inherently transitional character of gender, transsexuality needs to be considered as a psychic position in its own right in order to unveil its implications for psychoanalytic theories of gender formation.

Between burial and survival

Radical Hope engages the question of survival following a devastating conceptual collapse through Plenty Coups' ability to encounter enigma through loss. Once the act of planting coup-sticks became meaningless for a community who had lost its form of life, intelligibility was graspable only through a retroactive act of recounting and remembering the past. Indeed, recounting and remembering was a ritualistic act that gave meaning to the Crow Nation's history successes and failures, as culturally embedded "forms of insistence" (Lear, 2006, p. 34), which gave reality to the Crow's form of life. Lear here points to the paradox of collective experience: we have reality when we can "insist upon it" (Lear, 2006, p. 34), yet it is only through this insistence that reality itself takes its form. But if the meaning on which this insistence is grounded is lost, what remains? What could replace the planting coup-sticks? Or better, what happens when the signifying universe within which the ritual *means* breaks down? What would protect the tribe from disintegrating?

Remembering and recounting rituals in the aftermath of the catastrophic event of devastation experienced by the Crow may be viewed as a way to hold on to an idealized past. The repetitive act of recounting – in the double meaning of "narrating" and reenumerating – would constitute, from this perspective, a nostalgic form of memorialization expressing the tribe's melancholic attachment to their lost way of life, a refusal to let go. However, in a puzzling gesture during the burial of the Unknown Soldier in 1921, to which Plenty Coups was invited, he proceeded to bury his war bonnet along with his own coup-stick. While this act may be interpreted as a symbolic burial of the Crow's dead of a way of life, as a gesture of mourning and relinquishment, Lear points out that this act provides a crucial key to the question of survival after devastation. But how does Plenty Coups' burial of the coup-stick constitute, as Lear suggests, a prelude to hope? I here suggest that Plenty Coups' act of burial constituted a symbolic act akin to repression that transformed the coup-stick into a symbol of the past. Once the coup-stick was no longer upholded as the master signifier around which the tribe's cultural intelligibility was weaved, its burial and its ritualized retelling became the signifier of (re)founding loss that could make way into an unknown future. Significantly, in the aftermath of a catastrophe that Plenty Coups described as "the end of happenings", the act of burying the coup-stick constitutes a happening that inaugurates a new temporality.

As an act of repression, the burial of the coup-stick gives a renewed meaning to recounting and remembering. We may think here of narrating stories and remembering as acts of repetition that also attempt to signify loss, in the same way that the Fort/Da game signified for Freud an attempt to symbolize the mother's leaving. But the Fort/Da is the repression of the mother leaving, since it is the child who sends her away and brings her back. Through this game that represses the founding loss of the mother, the infant's agency is constituted. In this sense, one could argue that repression gives us grace and stops the repetition.

In the Fort/Da game the child is attempting to master a loss that happens in the present, and yet, the Fort/Da game signals the to-and-for movement of transitionality on which change and coming to terms with a past, depends. What must we bury in order to survive the collapse of gender as the paradigm of intelligibility through which we make sense of sexual difference? What must be repressed in the imaginary of gender is the phantasy of intelligibility, the certainty that blinds us to the fact that the object of our desire remains unknown and foreign to us. Repression is an act of deferral through a letting go and a bringing back, a letting go of the demand for the immediacy and certainty of satisfaction, a bringing back of such desire for satisfaction, which, through this very movement, through the rhythms of symbolic articulation, becomes transformed. Through this back and forth that simultaneously defers and differs (Derrida, 1982) temporality, a distinction between past, present and future emerges. Burying gender as an object of certainty means that we restructure our relation to our desire as something that remains foreign and unknown, as something that cannot be instructed upon since it is grounded in our imagination.

Can we imagine gender through the Fort/Da game as an act that crosses over the plane of identification with the Other; that traverses the phantasy of certainty and recognition? Imagining gender identification in this way means to treat it as a form of "holding" that allows for separation, that is, as a signification that inscribes its own resistance because its phantasized wholeness or unity is enjoyed precisely because of its impossibility. This kind of enjoyment depends on separating identification from the Other's desire (Pluth, 2007), on a point of "absolute difference" (Pluth, 2007, p. 131) where one's meanings can no longer rely on the meaning of the Other.

What does this formulation (Fort/Da) open for our thinking? In the Fort/Da, Freud is watching his grandson grapple with the absence of his mother. In analysis we put history back in time and tell a story that was not possible in the unfolding. We get caught in the unfolding as defense against trauma. Through enigmatic objects (interpretation, transsexuality, art) we find a notion of time that separates before, during and after. The enigma opens up what was fixed before. It leads to a "devastation" of what was known and places us in time, allows us to see something in the past that restructures our history. The scaffold has to be signified. Language does not simply wrack our omnipotence. We now have to find our way, to wonder what we want.

Sexual difference as dream

If we read Plenty Coups' story as a metaphor for the devastation of gender that this book invites us to consider, we may also consider the act of counting and remembering not only as repetition but also as an articulation of the enduring question of sexual difference. What resources might we draw upon to reach beyond the doxa of convention, to broaden the possibilities of meaning? For the Crow Nation it was a process of dream interpretation that allowed them to push conceptual limits. Dreams, Lear tells us, were treated as enigmatic objects – as reflections of wishes but also as authoritative guides as to whether their wishes would be granted. It was through a dream that Plenty Coups encountered a thread that would become a symbolic container for the catastrophic loss that his people had experienced. Plenty Coups' dream was treated as an enigmatic message rather than as a signifier of clarity and it is through this enigmatic quality that Lear imagines the axis of radical hope. The dream was not used to predict the future, and not unlike what happens in the analytic setting, it was presented to the tribe as a means to struggle with loss of intelligibility.

The dream has two parts. In the first part, Plenty Coups appears as a young boy struggling to decipher the dream's meaning. He is seated beside a "man-person" who is pointing to a hole in the ground from which scores of buffalo come out. The buffalo, however, don't look familiar, they are somehow unrecognizable, as if "from another world" (Lear, 2006, p. 70). In the second part of his dream Plenty Coups sees an old man and is told by the "man-person" that the old man is him, Plenty Coups. Then there is a storm that knocks down all the trees but one, that of the "chickadee-person". The chickadee-person, we are told, is a "good listener". He listens to people's stories of success and failure but he never intrudes, never misses a chance to learn from others (Lear, 2006, p. 90). Plenty Coups is told by the "man-person" in the dream that the chickadee survives by learning from others' successes and failures and then he is told to "develop [his] own mind"; "It is the mind that leads a man to power, not strength of body" (p. 71).

The tribe is able to treat the dream as an enigma despite the fact that the chickadee is identified as a bird who knows how to survive. The chickadee surprises us because it calls for an interpretation. The dreamer is asking "what are the virtues of the chickadee" (Lear, 2006, p. 147), and is able to use his imagination to transform and extend his understanding of courage beyond what it meant traditionally for a warrior culture of honour. Plenty Coups takes an analytic stance, that of interpretation, which is always fungible. The dream is treated as a soft object, to be pondered and played with, and yet, as a radically revelatory message capable of fracturing frozen chains of meaning and catalyzing the invention of new symbolic associations.

Lear shows us how treating loss as an enigma allowed Plenty Coups to draw upon the plasticity embedded in the fundamental cultural concepts that shape our way of life. The Crow Nation had lost "the concepts with which they would construct a narrative" (Lear, 2006, p. 32) and therefore, the acts of remembering and counting rituals, following the devastation, became a way to "locate" the loss in a new way – a form of working through that transformed the "destruction of a *telos* into a teleological suspension of the ethical" (Lear, 2006, p. 146). This transformation involved the paradoxical gesture of giving up the symbol of protection – the coup-stick – as a way to protect the Crow land. By giving up certitude, Plenty Coups was able to protect the unity and purpose of the Crow Nation, that is, to create an imagined link through which he and his people could survive discontinuity. The telling and retelling of this story functioned as a pathos of completion – the essence of Crow life that he was now able to pass on to future generations.

Plenty Coups' choices in the face of the inevitable devastation experienced by the Crow Nation poses questions regarding the possibility of the transformation of deeply engrained imaginaries of gender in our culture as well as of its implications. Cultures are bonded by fragile phantasies of homogeneity and they require an "authority foreign to the homogeneous" (Gasché, 1995, p. 161) to guarantee their stability, always under threat from the force of the heterogeneous. In Plenty Coups' narrative, the enigmatic message of the chickadee functions as such authority, which, like the position of the analyst, does not instruct. What Plenty Coups' story teaches us is that, provided that we keep on dreaming, losing our conception of gender does not mean losing the possibility of continuity and meaning. In understanding sexual difference as an enigmatic message that interpellates us without instructing us into gender; it can open the discontinuity of our history, the necessary incompleteness of every subject position and the instability of our sexuality to new imaginary unfoldings. Plenty Coups' position, as described by Lear, can be understood as a metaphor for the ways in which we struggle with the "reality" of sexual difference. His capacity to take advantage of the inherent plasticity of symbols allows him to face the reality of instability and heterogeneity. Plenty Coups understood only too well that the departure of the buffalo was final and, therefore, his wish for a return, of the buffalo, of the traditional way of life and its embedded ideal of human happiness had to be abandoned in order to restructure the very concepts through which to experience meaning and tradition: the very notion of what could count as happening.

If the gender ambiguity signified by transsexuality shatters our imaginary conception of gender, how would we recount, from a place of devastation, our history of becoming woman or man? How would we resignify femininity and masculinity in the face of the fragility of meaning and recognition?

The transsexual dream interpretation

Through Plenty Coups' dream, Lear helps us conceptualize history as a fractured story, as a re-counting and re-making of the past in the present that makes it intelligible, yet open to interpretation. What allows for this conceptual transformation is a space of vacancy created through an engagement with liminal objects outside of the everyday – dreams, art, the unconscious – all of which are soft, malleable objects that cannot be instructed into existence. The concept of transsexuality, too, can be conceptualized as a signifier for this liminal space that challenges the finitude of gender and calls for a different recounting of history, one that is ruptured, opaque, incomplete.

To imagine transsexuality as a metaphor for a liminal space we must consider the impossibility it signifies in the very wish for coherence it articulates. Transsexuality signifies a tension between enigma and concretization, wish and impossibility. It brings to mind both a desire for completion or intelligibility and the impossibility of that very wish. In this sense, it embodies the tension between wish fulfillment and repetition, the two defining aspects of dreaming and working through. In *Beyond the Pleasure Principle,* Freud (1920) articulates two significantly different dream theories (Levy, 2011, p. 129). In his second theory, trauma is said to disrupt psychic balance and this disruption is repeated in the dream as a way to master the anxiety, without regard for the law of the pleasure principle.

The traumatic dream can be understood both as wish fulfillment and repetition, combining manifest and latent contents in the weaving of the dream. There is a relationship between latent content and day residue where "Analysis of the dreamer's perceptions, feelings, fantasies and relations to the human figures in the dream assist in assessing the specific place of the dream-work in the construction and function of the dream" (Levy, 2011, p. 140).

For Levy, working through is bringing together the latent content and the day residue, linking the unmetabolized affect that accompanies, a left over of what had already happened, that is repeated in the current situation in therapy. Working through involves a repetition propelled by anxiety of a loss that had already happened. Only now, through taking the analytic position, that of interpretation, the repeated narrative is linked with the day residue, the "imaginary", through the transference. This conception of dream interpretation and working through as a combination of trauma and wish fulfillment (satisfaction and disruption) leans, I suggest, on what Freud called the "uncanny" and what we refer to, in this book, as enigma. The quality of the uncanny or of the enigma is undecidability, tension and murkiness. We can conceive of Freud's two dream theories, and Levy's conception of dream interpretation, as a combination of both theories that link "working through" to sexual difference. This link is possible if we consider sexual difference as the difference inherent to sexuality (Bass, 2000), that of the pulsating effect of time and timelessness, passivity and activity, pleasure and unpleasure, which leans upon a conception of primal time when the infant *is* the breast.

If the transference involves a return that also contains a wish fulfillment, the return is always incomplete: never the same. Traumatic repetition is an attempt to blur the difference within the self that is ironically grounded upon difference. Here we may return to Bass' (2000) formulation of the drive as an intrinsic push to differentiate along with a capacity or a curiosity that gains meaning only through relationships. Here it might be useful to return to the question we asked in the first chapter of this book: what happens to phantasy as it encounters not only the other's phantasy but one's phantasy about the other's phantasy? We may characterize the moment of interpretation as "transsexual"; that is, a moment when interpretation combines wish (day residue, concreteness) with traumatic repetition (disavowed affect). In the moment of interpretation, past and present, concrete experience and enigma, are indistinguishable and are linked through this flux of interpretation. The time of interpretation is both timeless and static; both future and past-oriented. Object and subject are conflated. The analyst is both a present object and the primal breast. Analyst and patient are linked in the differentiating erotic tension of the transference in a way that, as Bass (2006) points out, brings together self preservation and sexuality in primal time.

Turning a narrative to novel means changing the conception of what it means to have a gender through a return that relies on the concept's vacancy. It is an effect of radical hope that belongs to the analysis where concepts can be transgressed, played with and manipulated. The novel commentary on the narrative ushered by the enigma of analytic interpretation animates both the omnipotence of the Fort/Da act and its failure. It is a call for the imagination to open up different possibilities, to preserve some integrity in the face of history's discontinuity. The narrative is an attempt to master the trauma of loss and its resistance. It becomes a novel through the radical hope of imagination, through the ability to anticipate the emergence of that which may outstrip our capacity for understanding.

Pluth reminds us of Lacan's claim that signifiers are akin to puns in their ability to produce double meaning, when, for instance, unrelated words such as "familiar" and "millionaire" can be combined to create a nonsensical word like "famillionaire" that, none the less, "still manages to make sense" (Pluth, 2007, p. 108). It is in this way that I suggest we imagine gender embodiment: as reliant on a discourse that has preceded it but nevertheless constitutes an effect of that which is in excess of discourse. "Coming to gender", in short, is the idiosyncratic way one makes a *pun* on sedimented social discourse through the shock of subjective experience, grounded as it is on the enigmatic course of desire.

A return to art

Kapoor's art forces us, the spectators, to glimpse and experience the after effect of trauma, the Fort/Da created by the registration of difference between what Bhaba characterizes as "the physicality of void space and truly made emptiness" (2011, p. 178). Void and presence become united by difference or, better, void and presence create each other through difference. The Fort/Da of the narrative, like the movement in Kapoor's pieces, creates a sort of "doubling" – a displacement that prevents us from registering the object as whole. If the gendered body too can be imagined as container for its polar opposites – negative, positive, absence, presence – then narrating gender is a form of embroidery of the experienced body and its otherness; its fullness and its void, an act-in-process carried on between representation and its failure.

Subjecting gender to analysis also means tolerating its death. What is lost is the concept's adhesive attachment to its form (male/female) and the phantasy of its stability. If, as Bass (2000) suggests, sexuality is traumatic, it is a trauma that pushes us to both separate and unite. Putting trauma into words, narrating our own sexuality is difficult and yet, it is only through language that sexuality is sustained as an enigmatic message from and to the other and whose content is dispersed "away from bodily actions" (Britzman, 2011, p. 3). For the narrative of gender to become novel, a re-writing of one's terms of intelligibility, it must remain unfixed, inexhaustible, and the subject must be willing to defer/differ the desire for gratification.

Like a prophesy, gender is handed to us at birth enveloped in pre-determined meanings. "Are we male or female?" is a question that the adult rarely asks, not because it cannot be settled, but because it is felt to be answered. The vagueness of identification and the unconscious object of desire, which is always genderless, breaks through in retrospect presenting an enigma that can be either settled concretely, through an attack on linking and desire or, instead, can help transition thinking itself. To think with, through and against gender means to face the question of loss through the inhibition of the polymorphous nature of sexuality that predicates its existence. Lived and understood as a phantasy of intelligible embodiment, gender shields us from the pain of loss, from the anxiety of the unknown, but in its fixedness, the fluid and heterogeneous character of sexuality, which is always in transit, dissipates as well.

In thinking of gender through enigmatic objects we manage to displace the origin of gender because the question of originality, in gender as well as in art, is always "pre-fabricated" (Bhaba, 2011, p. 64). Art objects are uncertain and unsettling, and similarly to the transsexual body, can be given sacred meanings, become idealized or seen as abject emblems of uncanny indeterminacy (Kristeva, 1982). Like the mirrors in Kapoor's sculptures, transsexuality does not only reflect the enigma of gender and its indeterminate origin but, more importantly, it also unsettles the very notion of gender and displaces the axis on which gender intelligibility rests. When the questions of origin and authenticity become irrelevant to gender, the enigma of sexual difference gives way to questions of creativity and imagination. We allow ourselves to be split open, to be effected and affected by ever shifting meaning across a non-hierarchical "field of objects" (Bhabha, 2011, p. 64). It is this "lateral" approach to the psychic movement that establishes new semiotic links. In being conceived as continual approximation, the concept of gender loses its preordained meaning as whole or autonomous. By framing gender as both an enigma and a reinvented solution to the enigma of sexuality, it can be finally dislodged from questions of identity (male/female) because what it represents is the tension between known and unknown, self and other, holding place and rupture of subjectivity.

The constitutional struggle for the subject of trying to live a life s/he does not fully understand is an act linked with taking a stance in gender. Understood in this way, gender is also an imaginative tool that can help us deal with devastation when its potential to shape the subject's particular history is realized. If engenderment is "a giving form to absence" – the always already irretrievable lost object – we can think about one's life narration as a process of engenderment – that is, as a simultaneous process of coming to gender/coming to being – as an endless insistence on making meaning of an impossibility. Gender constitutes both a disruption and a solution to the trauma that founds subjectivity, an attempt at bridging an irreducible gap that propels for closure. Yet, when considered through this imaginative pun, a signifier holding in tension presence and absence, becoming gendered constitutes a poetic bridging through which the subject can author her/his one desire.

The trans-sexuality of thinking and memory

For Plenty Coups, taking an imaginative stance entailed letting go of the desire to know, to settle the dream's enigma in the form of revenge or war. Understanding the dream as a hint, an approximation, a message that addresses but does not instruct, Plenty Coups' interpretation suggests a giving into a transitional form of experience, a space of latency, a waiting for thoughts to emerge. Within this paradoxical state of abeyance that tolerates the loss of framing concepts and identity coordinates, Plenty Coups gives the Crow Nation the opportunity to restructure a new sense of what counts as living meaningfully, that is, of embedding themselves once again in "an imaginative-desiring-erotic-honor-seeking life" (Lear, 2006, p. 15).

I want to return here to my session with Sam to consider the relation between intelligibility and desire. We may recall that Sam, a female to male, states with excitement: "I want to be a man that dresses in women's clothing. I like fucking up with people's minds." He expresses a deep ambiguity regarding the idea of staying in his female body and wearing men's clothes because "they are boring. Not me". He also says, "I am disgusted by my 'growths'" (breasts). Sam wants to be unintelligible to the other; he doesn't want to be either a man or a woman but to remain undecipherable to the other. His position appears to be reactive, not because of his desire to remain unintelligible, but because his narrative is still caught in the discourse of the other and dislodged from self-meaning.

I understand Sam's grievance as a difficulty in giving up the wish of non-difference through taking a stance in gender. The issue here is not one of adaptation to cultural signifiers of femininity and masculinity that would make him intelligible to the other but rather his inability to position himself in gender as a subject of desire, that is, from the recognition of the impossibility of satisfaction. Ironically, Sam has difficulties assuming a transsexual stance, taking a hold of and announcing his desire, since this self-positioning would entail the renunciation of complete satisfaction. The prohibition that Sam experiences as coming from the outside – you cannot be both a man and a woman – which is read as an attack on his being, prevents him from accessing his internal identification with absence, his refusal to occupy a position from which to desire from. Sam's stance ensures that he cannot be seen at the same time that he demands attention. Feeling caught in the discourse of the other while simultaneously refusing to occupy a position from which his desire could be experienced and read, Sam feels stuck in a non-place that makes him feel both encroached upon and invisible.

Announcing one's desire entails a movement from signification to expression. The analytic process opens up one's discourse for grazing when the analyst glides through the patient's narrative and listens to the metaphors, slips of the tongue and negations through which discourse becomes speech, the moments at which the subject's lack shows through, the very lack that sutures the subject to discourse. Sam's difficulty in taking a stance in gender is enacted through attempts to confuse and provoke the other, an idealized other that both traps and denies him recognition. Who is Sam genderless for? Is his wish to be a boy for his mother and a girl for his father? Between a gender interpellation that makes Sam invisible and his own difficulty in taking a hold of his desire lies the analytical space, a threshold, a transition into a self-authored form of imaginative, desiring and erotic engenderment.

The transsexual future of an illusion

If gender ceases to make sense – like the ritual of counting coup-sticks for the Crow tribe – the difference between the signifiers "man" and "woman" becomes a riddle. Just as Lear observes in regard to the loss of a way of life, a transition toward a new understanding of gender requires a shift in our conception of time. Temporality constitutes a certain form of order, and it is through the notions of before and after that we give meaning to the passing of time. The encounter with other forms of embodiment that challenge gender's intelligibility also empties gender of its temporality: at the moment of loss of gender coordinates, the body falls into an abyss, incomprehensible and unmovable. Once predetermined notions of masculinity and femininity fail, questions that did not make sense before can now be asked: what is a man? What is a woman? Some of the art pieces that we have examined through this book hold these questions in their undecipherability and invite us to consider their forgotten enigmatic nature as we struggle with dilemmas of recognition and knowledgeability which are essential to gender and identity.

The notion that there are only two sexes, apparently confirmed by the raw immediacy of anatomy, is always in conflict with our psychic experience of sexual difference. As Dean argues, "despite the abundance of cultural representations of differences between the sexes, the unconscious does not get it" (2000, p. 86). It is this space of indeterminacy that the transsexual body comes to signify and that it compels us to disentangle while simultaneously forcing a constant displacement from decipherment to approximation. In experiencing anew the enigma of sexual difference, the certainty of knowledge dissolves and we are forced to confront our inescapable dependency and passivity. The analytic space offers us the opportunity to give into this experience of dependency and passivity through the work of interpretation, the encounter with the elusiveness of meaning, and the fragility of knowledge that fractures rigid idealizations and repetitions. Our patients' stream of associations reveal phantasies of cohesion and mastery, unity and plenitude, but they also reveal the pulsating force of desire in their narrative's fissures, contradictions and aporias. Analysis, like art objects, holds in tension what is irreducible and inexhaustible, the enigmas of gender, time, otherness, sexuality and memory, turning narratives into novels through a re-telling and re-linking of fragments in time. The existence of the unconscious makes the questions "am I a man or woman?" and "where do I end and the other begins?" unanswerable. But to raise questions in the absence of given truths opens up the possibility of temporary and fragmentary answers that provide fleeting pleasure or rest on transient experiences of wish fulfillment and illusion. In the enigmatic encounter that is the analysis experience a space may open between the concreteness of the wish and the emptiness of the word-container in order to create both a loss of concepts and richer associative links.

For the transsexual patient, the process of transitioning may be experienced as a sort of rupture where, after numerous and extensive surgeries, "nothing happens" and one is left split and incomplete. Rarely a moment of resolution, sex reassignment surgery may paradoxically signal the beginning of transitioning, the creation of a ground for self-authorship and imaginative recreation. It is important to notice that there is not one, unique meaning that can be assigned to the process of transitioning and even for the same individual, transitioning is an event with changing meanings and implications over time. Indeed, narratives about transitioning may be framed as forgetting of one's past, a retelling that restructures one's relation to oneself or as a process of mourning of the impossibility of achieving a sense of completeness through transitioning.

As I have argued throughout this book, gender identification is not only a question for the transsexual (or other transgendered individuals). Known, unknown and presumed to be known, gender is a complex construction that amalgamates old familial interpellations, sedimented bodily sensations along orifices and erotogenic zones, the history of our desire and accidental identifications. Taking a stance in gender is a universal challenge, not a problem for a few individuals. The clinical vignettes from S's and Sam's case-stories show that the way in which we come to understand our gender is a matter of life and death. For some, the search for an identity that one can live in, with, and toward requires grazing against limited and injurious gender formulations, a process through which the insufficiency of such categories is made transparent for every subject. Through the work of analytic interpretation, which calls for a narrative that links the unintelligibility of trauma to what is other to it, a comprehensible event that can be communicated to the other and to the otherness of the self, the rigidity of such formulations may be lessened in the hopes that we can soften our hold on gender. This act of hope joins the analytic process and gender as radical holding spaces for creativity and desire; radical, because to hold new transitional spaces for embodying gender otherwise requires that our traditional understanding of sexual difference undergo devastating transitions.

Lear understands radical hope as an awaiting for something one lacks appropriate concepts to understand (2006, p. 103). It is a hope for the emergence of a subjectivity that does not yet exist. This hope is grounded on the recognition that we are finite desiring beings and that we respond to this finitude with imagination. Our subjectivity is defined by and is inconstant with a struggle with otherness and the foreignness of our sexuality, which pushes us to narrate at the same time that it ruptures our narrative, making us vulnerable by exposing the limits of language and imagination. The paradox of subjectivity lies in the fact that our eroticism makes us infinite and yet this very infinity is grounded on lack. If courage is the ability to live well within the limitations and risks of human existence, it means then to dare inhabit and embrace our finite erotic nature as always lacking, never completely satisfied beings. As a commitment to pathos, courage pushes us to hold in tension a narrative that bridges eroticism and infinity, sexuality and culture.

Conclusion
Afterwordness

What comes after transitioning? If the road to a solution is filled with anxiety, what happens after a solution is created? I suggest that we begin with these questions to make our own transitioning possible. Just as with Cal, the survival of our psychic space as analysts and analysands begins with a re-telling – a process of sidestepping and interruption to a seeming linearity. Analysis teaches us to look at objects diagonally, from the side, as if from a third eye, creating a space of emptiness, an enigma that linearity forecloses. A similar lesson is found in art. Kapoor's installations, whose presence Bhabha describes as ubiquitous (2011, p. 180), place the spectator in transition, interrupting her ongoing history. Looking at gender from this diagonal space opens its elusive qualities, which allow us to turn gender into our own finding/creation. We are reminded, through this fractured look, that identification is always partial, always conflictual, and so gender too has this doubling effect. We may say that gender, like the unconscious, shows us only glimpses and flashes of our being. What emerges as presence or as day-residue is simply a gathering point that conceals as much as it reveals. Like memory, gender gives the appearance of wholeness but it is made up of the material of phantasy, which can never be stabilized in time.

The question of intelligibility and memory is invoked in Lyotard's discussion of the inevitability and impossibility of discourse (2011). There is a kind of violence in universality, which, Lyotard suggests, is inherent in discourses of otherness – our reception of meaning in discourse is always somewhat passive since our symbolic existence depends on this shared meaning without which discourse's otherness would manifest as terror coming from without. The collapse of the possibility of meaningful communication returns us to the brutality of essentialism. Discourse wraps itself around us as a protective illusion. It acts both as ground for desire and its obstacle, since we signify our desire via discourse and yet, discourse itself is shaped by the unconscious, making its meaning fragmentary and ever shifting.

Considering discourse as both inevitable and impossible places memory at a similar junction. Memory is not fully determined by discourse because discourse itself expresses something that can only be grazed against or seen partially: an unsignified core that cannot be articulated in language. This conceptualization of discourse as a phantasm effected by the Real allows us to think of identification and embodiment as endless processes of becoming into which we can only gain partial access through a kind of "grazing" (Lyotard, 2011, p. 9).

The psychoanalysis act is akin to what Bhabha describes as a feature of Kapoor's work in that it performs "a distinction between the didacticism of 'expression' and the divination of 'bringing to expression'" (Bhabha, 2011, p. 187). Both the analytic act and the work of art open discourse to its emptiness and timelessness, revealing its inherent instability. In referring to one of Kapoor's installations titled "Void", Bhabha writes:

> And then suddenly – with respect to the void – in the emptiness that holds the rock, I see a ghost. It doesn't rise; nor does it descend. It does not allow the eye to seek the satisfaction of origin. Does it come from within? from without?. . . It is, once more, the movement of the material *in and through* the non-material, the ghost *in and out* of the stone, that gives the work its character: like Hamlet's father, *Ghost* walk the night, wafting us to a more "removed ground".
>
> (Bhabha, 2011, p. 181).

Bhabha reminds us here that the object can never be captured. The ground is always unstable, shaking and creating repetitive ripples that make "the eye hover horizontally, homeless" (Bhabha, 2011, p. 181).

Kapoor's "Void" forces us to recognize that carving an identity is not a process of configuration that takes place in relation to absolute presence or absence but, rather, at the contradictory juncture where absence and presence unite, where the eye absorbs an image while simultaneously registering its blind spot. Analysis too relies on this knowledge of the negative. Negation captures the said and the not-said, the present and its obverse. Like gender, analysis does not reveal truth but reassembles and blurs narratives and images, and in this sense, it constitutes an act of "voiding" (Bhabha, 2011, p. 183) that empties history of its ideality. The truth that is created in the process, when opened to its otherness, no longer appears as sedimented past. Its materiality becomes "living tissue" (2011, p. 184), to borrow Bhabha's words, enabling us "to make something else possible" (Bhabha, 2011, p. 184) when it is approached as a "contingent and relational medium" (2011, p. 184). Similarly, through the analytic act, the gendered body becomes a tenuous creation when it is treated as an esthetic object. Bringing sexuality, which is outside time, to affect the pathos of one's narrative means that gender too is always in flux, between the imaginary and the imagination.

If sexuality, like the object of art, is always out of balance "pushing and pulling out . . . back and forth" (Bhabha, 2011, p. 185) then gender too – as a signifier of lack, a veiled "thing", a blind spot – is both inside and outside of time. Gender can only encircle the lost object but never fill out the void. Through its blind spots, it discloses "the transitional state of true making" (2011, p.185), as Bhabha beautifully puts it. Thinking of the transsexual body as an analytic object allows us to reveal the shaky ground of sexuality and gender, and not unlike the spectator's eye as it encounters the enigmatic art object, to expand our field of vision when our mind's eye is pushed and pulled, back and forth, "side by side". Understood as a narrative that unites divergent temporalities, gender performs a "transition between the perceptual and conceptual" (Bhabha, 2011, p. 186), becoming a sort of a "gathering place", which like the sculpture's stone is "not about the stone but about something else . . . it is part of a circulatory exchange of difference and similitude, the repetition of the shape and the revision of the sign, that is peculiar to objects in transition" (Bhabha, 2011, p. 186). The transsexual body is a reminder of the fullness and emptiness of embodiment, of the obliquity of the body's present: a trace of the primal past, yet also of the future, in transition.

This is why writing about gender is a difficult task. What is produced through this writing is a text that carries the enigma inherent in gender: the wish to foreclose, to explain, to give words while in full awareness of the impossibility of exhausting its meaning. The difference that gender signifies is both concealed and revealed in and through writing. In analysis too, the enigma of gender is located at the core of the analytic experience. The closer we get to our "body of knowledge" the more we disentangle knowledge from our body in such a way that we come to think of *every body* as a precarious space, present in relation to time, yet primal. In analysis, we conceptualize our body as a non-object, as "the taking place" of embodiment.

Throughout this book, I have elaborated on the ways in which transsexuality sows deep doubts into our conception of gender, shaking our presumed mastery over sexuality and the body. We have seen how the concept of transitioning compels us to see our bodies as uncanny and enigmatic. A recurrent question throughout this book has been about the ethics of psychoanalysis in relation to its defensive stance vis-a-vis gender. Since the question of making meaning and assuming subjectivity is negotiated through the analytic process, we must ask ourselves: what is the ethical stance that psychoanalytic practice depends upon? Do we listen with the intention of helping patients adapt to larger social structures, which the analyst comes to represent, or do we participate in a creative construction of psychic space? How relevant is the clinic in terms of understanding social structures and political life? I have argued that psychoanalytic ethics requires us to limit ourselves to the question of how people live their lives or get caught in the imaginary. The more important questions to psychoanalysis are those that allow us to search and create and, therefore, I argue, that the question of transsexual surgery should shift from one of "reassignment" to one of "transitioning". Transitioning opens up a new discourse of agency and care that takes time to develop.

Through case examples, I have argued that psychoanalysis should treat symptoms (e.g. gender oscillation) as attempts at "working through" rather than as obstacles. The predicament of choosing one's gender manifests as a conflict that expresses itself in the patient's family and work life, and in a series of other scenes through which we glimpse the ways individuals mediate between inner and outer reality. From this perspective, the gender question can be approached as a form of signal anxiety – characteristic of repetition compulsion – that prevents confrontation with difference within the self.

Still, the question of re-assignment surgery is often invoked in some psychoanalytic narratives as the signifier for the foreclosure of the symbolic and, therefore, for the psychotic organization of the transsexual (e.g. Chiland, 2005; Millot, 1990; Wolff-Bernstein, 2011). The transsexual, it is often argued, wishes to change his sex but, in mistaking sex for genitalia, he fails to change his position in relation to jouissance. In this narrative, the transsexual condition is considered to be grounded on the error of confusing gender and jouissance and on the failure to enter the symbolic register. Lacan's conceptualization of the mirror stage, for example, has been used as a means to question the psychic stability of the transsexual, since the disenchantment of the transsexual with his or her body is assumed to relate to the failure of the transsexual to identify with his or her image. As a Lacanian analyst speaking at a recent conference claimed, the transsexual knows no jouissance of the body, only that of the flesh, which is not symbolic.

What is problematic about this position is that it forgets that identity emerges through the mirror stage as a retroactive construct. It forgets that the infant's feeling of jubilation depends on the mother's holding, which the infant misreads as his own mastery. In a similar way, the insistence on equating transsexuality with psychotic "certainty" forgets that no one escapes the imaginary of gender and that each individual analysis concerns the question of "what is the state of *this* imaginary" (Gozlan, 2011a), which is tied to the specificity of the unconscious. We must not forget that by the time one wonders about and elects surgery, a number of questions have been already raised: what am I willing to lose? What am I willing to change? What new possibilities are open to me? What new anxieties lay ahead? How will I be happy? These are all important and productive questions that may engender psychic transformation. But the existential truth is that no one knows what the experience of transitioning means until it is undergone and so we need to understand that transitioning cannot have a univocal meaning.

One may ask, what is the concretizing certainty that psychoanalysis clutches on to? Holding on to the enigma of sexuality is difficult, and even psychoanalysis fails at its own decentring. Psychoanalysis, as any other discourse, cannot resist being affected by its own trauma. As psychoanalysis itself reminds us, decentring is always partial and so my only hope is to contribute to current efforts to destabilize our deep investment in certainty and knowledge. We may be reminded here of Derbyshire's insistence that "Psychoanalytic interpretation must emerge from a dialogue with the patient and the dialogic relation of the speech genre that is the analytic, exerts a form of resistance to the wilder form of speculation" (2010, p. 88). He warned:

> When wider cultural phenomena are taken as objects of psychoanalytic investigation, that is, when such phenomena are read *symptomatically,* controls and reciprocity are lost, and the object becomes amenable to an unlimited semiosis: there is no resistance to meaning evoked by the researcher, who now acts as an untrammelled interpreter.
>
> (Derbyshire, 2010 p. 88)

The assertion that transsexual surgery is an act that excludes the symbolic is grounded on the suspect idea that there is a pure, authentic body that should be "left to nature" and that the transsexual, in his demand for surgery, disrupts. The story of the Crow tribe reminds us, however, that nature is thoroughly implicated within the social and, in the case of transsexuality, technology. There is no pure nature that is disrupted by sociality, no natural desire that is outside of culture.

The question of the relation of transsexuality to psychosis, which, as we have seen, is invoked by many analysts (Chiland, 2005; Millot, 1990; Wolff-Bernstein, 2011; among others), is based on the idea that, since transitioning often takes form on the flesh, the transsexual subject cannot identify with the jouissance of the image. This assumption reveals a hyper-culturalization of sexuality in some Lacanian approaches to transsexuality. Freud reminds us, however, of the interconnectedness of phantasy and reality in our experience of the ego as bodily surface. Even for the psychotic there is an effort to bring these realms – imaginary, symbolic and the Real – together. As Cal, Herculine, Sam and S show us, the transsexual disenchantment with her body cannot be situated in any particular register because it is a question of *the relation* between the symbolic, the real, and the imaginary.

What the equation of transsexuality with psychosis reveals is a purist understanding of nature as fixed and unmodifiable. We may ask ourselves, however, if it is transsexuality that cannot enter the symbolic or if we are dealing here with a larger problem involving culture's own fractured symbolic that denies the polymorphous perversity of sexuality. If we follow Lacanian theorizations of language in its relation to the unconscious, the thorough and a priori interconnectedness of the real, symbolic and imaginary registers becomes apparent: Any modifications on the body – including cosmetic surgery, or ear piercing – involve the "real" of the flesh, but no intervention on the body can possibly exclude its imaginary and symbolic meanings and connotations. Therefore, to claim that a particular act forecloses the symbolic is to treat the imaginary, symbolic and the real as discrete entities. Such an approach denies the inseparability of the three registers and hence the murky nature of experience, even of the psychotic experience.

Is psychoanalysis – as opposed to psychiatry or psychology – not interested in the effort involved and the capacity to live without falling apart or giving up? If so, why shouldn't we consider the possibility of surgery as a radical intervention that is also an act of hope or an expression of the transformative nature of the human? If we agree that psychical life is determined by a force that we can't fully know, how do we link our desires to our always limited and contingent choices and how we live creatively with the symptom? This is the question that Plenty Coups' radical approach brings to the question of how to live with psychic and cultural devastation. It shows us that what saves us from ourselves is always bigger than ourselves, that it is through an anticipation of something not yet known that we invent our subjectivity.

As I have shown, an aesthetic approach to the question of transsexuality allows us to reconsider surgery as a possibility of representing oneself comfortably in the world as well as of shifting one's relations to one's internal objects. Like the encounter with an enigmatic object, surgery is a new beginning – we do not know what will happen afterwards and what possibilities will be opened or foreclosed. In other words, we must have radical hope in order to uphold psychoanalytic ethics.

Scintillation between two deaths (Barthes, 2011, p. 55)

As any other act, transsexual surgery can be experienced as a form of manic triumph. However, it is crucial that we consider the fact that the transsexual subject's intense occupation with transitioning dissipates as life goes on after surgery. I suggest that transitioning does not begin nor end with surgery.

As a metaphor for the polymorphism of desire, transsexuality conveys the tension of psychic difference through a process, that of transitioning, which opens us to the dilemma of gender. Transitioning is both an attempt to represent a gap within the self and a reproduction of this gap. Through transitioning, our bodies become aesthetic objects that take shape between two deaths: the loss of what we never had and wish to regain, and the death that occurs at the moment of apprehension of the illusion of having. Words can only brush against meaning and cannot guarantee recognition or understanding. As writers we wonder, who am I writing/speaking to? This is also a question that can be asked about our gender: what am I to the Other? Reading and being read become one and the same thing: an encounter with our own otherness. This other that reads us always embodies a kernel of the self and returns as otherness to whom we desperately attempt to convey intelligibility or hide in obscurity.

If writing is a form of engenderment, this book also carries the enigmas, conflicts, lack and excess that intertwine in the threshold between body and psyche. Reader and writer also meet at this strange and estranged place between representation and excess, aesthetics and concreteness. Reader and writer are situated as analysands in relation to the enigmatic text because the closer we get to the enigmatic object of our desire, the more incomplete and fractured it appears, forcing us to lean on the imagination to fill in the gap.

In analysis, our narrative becomes a novel through the radical hope of the imagination: the ability to tolerate waiting for something to emerge that may outstrip our capacity for understanding. Gender, as a conceptual resource, acts as a "bridge" that links our finite eroticism to the infinity of our desire. While gender cannot be fully filled with knowledge and, therefore, incites in us a desire for a totalizing and final answer, it also functions as a narrative; it is also an act of hope.

Herculine Barbin showed us what happens when the option of transsexuality is closed off in culture, when the hope for our psyche to transition is foreclosed. Calliope's character, on the other hand, provides an example of the aporia that subjectivity emerges only when there is a fracture, a gap between psyche and culture. For Calliope, the dichotomy of gender becomes de-literalized through a lie that exposes the instability of discourse and opens gender to the enigma of sexuality. For Cal, deception functions as a productive side-stepping through which he transitions the way he listens to the Other. In treating transsexuality and gender as enigmatic objects, we have also side-stepped the edges of our fantasy, thus opening our own certainty to the pathos of imagination.

As readers, we have come to situate ourselves in a murky place, blurring the gap between observers and creators of art. Not unlike analysands caught in the midst of transference, the reader's own sexuality disrupts his or her reading, conflating phantasy and reality. From this place we, as readers and writers of our experience, must also ask ourselves: is our narrative a sort of lie that keeps a gap between the self and the Other? How do we listen to our patients' "lies"? Can we transition our own listening in a way that maintains the enigma of difference? Bringing together enigmatic art objects and transsexuality, we are left with a set of questions through which to take distance from the certainties of gender, and we are reminded that it is through this "taking distance" that the seeming cacophony of odd objects may turn into composition. It is this distance from the authority of knowledge that is required of psychoanalysis so that it can give up its captivation with its own mirror image and continue to reinvent itself.

References

Adams, M. (2007). *Self and social change.* London: Sage.
Adams, P. (1996). *The emptiness of the image: Psychoanalysis and sexual difference.* New York: Routledge.
Ambrosio, G. (Ed.). (2009). *Transvestism, transsexualism in the psychoanalytic dimension.* London: Karnac Books.
Barthes, R. (2011). *The preparation of the novel.* (Columbia University Press, Trans.). New York: Columbia University Press.
Bass, A. (2000). *Difference and disavowal: The trauma of eros.* Stanford, CA: Stanford University Press.
Bass, A. (2006). *Interpretation and difference: The strangeness of care.* Stanford, CA: Stanford University Press.
Bataille, G. (2001). *The story of the eye.* (D. Bergelson, Trans.). San Francisco: City Lights Publishers.
Benjamin, J. (1998). *Shadow of the other: Intersubjectivity and gender in psychoanalysis.* New York: Routledge.
Bhabha, H. (2011). *Anish Kapoor.* Paris: Flammarion.
Bollas, C. (1987). *The shadow of the object.* London: Free Association Books.
Breuer, J., & Freud, S. (1974). On the psychical mechanism of hysterical phenomena: Preliminary communication. In J. Strachey (Ed. & Trans.), *The standard edition of the complete psychological works of Sigmund Freud* (Volume 2, pp. 3–17). London: Hogarth Press. (Original work published 1893).
Britzman, D. P. (2006). *Novel education: Psychoanalytic studies on learning and not learning.* New York: Peter Lang.
Britzman, D. P. (2009). *The very thought of education: Psychoanalysis and the impossible professions.* Albany, NY: State University of New York Press.
Britzman, D. P. (2011). *Freud and education.* New York: Routledge.
Britzman, D. P. (2011, November). On the difficulties of representing sexuality in research, politics, and education (keynote). In Conference *Sexuality and Education.* Conference conducted at University of Buenos Aires, Buenos Aires, Argentina.
Britzman, D. P. (2012). The adolescent teacher: A psychoanalytic note on regression in the professions. *Journal of Infant, Child, and Adolescent Psychotherapy,* 11 (3), 272–283.
Britzman, D. P. (Forthcoming). An imaginative dialogue between H. G. Adler and psychoanalysis: Aesthetic themes of uncertainty, transformation, and binding. In J. Creet, S. Horowitz, & A. Dan. (Eds.), *H.G. Adler: Life, literature and legacy.* Evanston, IL: Northwestern University Press.

Britzman, D. P. (n.d.). *The return of "The Question Child": Reading "Ma Vie en Rose" through Melanie Klein.* Retrieved November 20, 2013, from http://www.academyanalyticarts.org/britzman.htm.

Butler, J. (1990). *Gender trouble: Feminism and the subversion of identity.* New York: Routledge.

Chiland, C. (2005). *Exploring transsexualism.* (D. Alcorn, Trans.). London: Karnac.

Copjec, J. (2004). *Imagine there's no woman: Ethics and sublimation.* Cambridge: MIT Press.

Dean, T. (2000). *Beyond sexuality.* Chicago: The University of Chicago Press.

De Certeau, M. (1988). *The writing of history.* (T. Conley, Trans.). New York: Columbia University Press.

Derbyshire, P. (2010). Unlimited semiosis: The problem of researching culture psychoanalytically in Tim Dean's unlimited intimacy. *Sitegeist,* 5, (Winter), 87–99.

Derrida, J. (1982). *Margins of philosophy.* (A. Bass, Trans.). Chicago: University of Chicago Press.

Derrida, J. (1998). *Resistances of psychoanalysis.* (P. Kamuf, P. A. Brault & M. Naas, Trans.). Stanford, CA: Stanford University Press.

Dimen, M. (2003). *Sexuality, intimacy, power.* Hillsdale, MI: Analytic Press.

Efrati, D., & Israeli, Y. (2007). *The philosophy and psychoanalysis of Jacques Lacan.* Jerusalem: Ministry of Defense.

Eigen, M. (2009). *Flames from the unconscious: Trauma, madness and faith.* London: Karnac.

Ettinger, B. (2002). Weaving a trans-subjective tress or the matrixial sinthome. In L. Thurston (Ed.), *Reinventing the symptom: Essays on the final Lacan* (pp. 83–109). New York: Other Press.

Eugenides, J. (2002). *Middlesex.* Toronto: Random House.

Fachinelli, E. (2007). On the beach. *Journal of European Psychoanalysis, 24.* Retrieved March 20, 2014 from http://www.psychomedia.it/jep/number24/facchinelli.htm.

Fink, B. (1995). *The Lacanian subject: Between language and jouissance.* Princeton, NJ: Princeton University Press.

Fletcher, J., & Benjamin, A. E. (Eds). (1990). *Abjection, melancholia, and love: The work of Julia Kristeva.* New York: Routledge.

Foucault, M. (1980). *Herculine Barbin.* (R. McDougall, Trans.). New York: Vintage Books.

Freud, S. (1974a). Beyond the pleasure principle. In J. Strachey (Ed. and Trans.), *The standard edition of the complete psychological works of Sigmund Freud* (Vol. 18, pp. 1–64). London: Hogarth Press. (Original work published 1920).

Freud, S. (1974b). Three essays on the theory of sexuality. In J. Strachey (Ed. and Trans.), *The standard edition of the complete psychological works of Sigmund Freud* (Vol. 7, pp. 125–248). London: Hogarth Press. (Original work published 1905).

Freud, S. (1974c). Wild psychoanalysis. In J. Strachey (Ed. and Trans.), *The standard edition of the complete psychological works of Sigmund Freud* (Vol. 11, pp. 221–227). London: Hogarth Press. (Original work published 1910).

Freud, S. (2006). Note on the "Magic Notepad". In A. Philips (Ed.), *The Penguin Freud reader* (pp. 101–105). London: Penguin. (Original work published 1925).

Gasché, R. The Heterological Almanac. (L. A. Boldt-Irons, Trans.). In L. A. Boldt-Irons (Ed.), *On Bataille: Critical essays* (pp. 157–208). Albany, NY: State University of New York Press.

Gherovici, P. (2010). *Please select your gender: From the invention of hysteria to the democratizing of transgenderism.* New York: Routledge.

Gozlan, O. (2008). The accident of gender. *Psychoanalytic Review, 95*(4), 541–70.

Gozlan, O. (2010). The "Real" time of gender. *European Journal of Psychoanalysis,* 30, 61–84.

Gozlan, O. (2011a). The tenderness of gender meets the harshness of the psychoanalytic clinic. *Other/Wise, 1,* 4–5. Retrieved March 20, 2014 from http://ifpe.wordpress.com/2012/12/01/the-tenderness-of-gender-meets-the-harshness-of-the-psychoanalytic-clinic/

Gozlan, O. (2011b). Transsexual surgery: A novel reminder and a navel remainder. *International Forum of Psychoanalysis,* 20 (1), 45–52.

Green, A. (2002). *Time in psychoanalysis: Some contradictory aspects.* (A. Weller, Trans.). London: Free Association Books.

Grossman, D. (2011). *Falling out of time.* The New Library, Ha Kibutz Ha Meuchad.

Grosz, E. (2001). The strange detours of sublimation: Psychoanalysis, homosexuality, and art. *Umbr(a): Polemos,* 141–154.

Hardaker, J. (2012). *Review: Anish Kapoor, MCA Sydney.* Retrieved December 20, 2013 from http://megaphoneoz.com/?p=3187.

Harris, A. (2002). Gender as contradiction. In M. Dimen, & V. Goldner (Eds.), *Gender in psychoanalytic space: Between clinic and culture.* New York: Other Press.

Harris, A. (2005). *Gender as soft assembly.* Hillsdale, MI: The Analytic Press.

Heidegger, M. (1966). Conversation on a country path about thinking (J. M. Anderson & E. H. Freund, Trans.). In *Discourse on thinking* (pp. 58–90). New York: Harper Torchbooks.

Hornzee-Jones, C. (2010). Engineering the art of Anish Kapoor. In *Anish Kapoor: Memory* (pp. 88–93). New York: Guggenheim Museum Publication.

Johnston, A. (2005). *Time driven: Metapsychology and the splitting of the drive.* Evanston, IL: Northwestern University Press.

Kristeva, J. (1982). *Powers of horror: An essay on abjection.* (L. S. Roudiez, Trans.). New York: Columbia University Press.

Kristeva, J. (1991). *Strangers to ourselves.* (L. S. Roudiez, Trans.). New York: Columbia University Press.

Kristeva, J. (1996). *Time and sense: Proust and the experience of literature.* (R. Guberman, Trans.). New York: Columbia University Press.

Kristeva, J. (2002). *Intimate revolt: The powers and the limits of psychoanalysis.* (J. Herman, Trans.). New York: Columbia University Press.

Kristeva, J. (2007). Adolescence: A syndrome of ideality. (M. Marder & P. Vieira, Trans.). *Psychoanalytic Review,* 94 (5), 716–725.

Kristeva, J. (2010). *Hatred and forgiveness.* (J. Herman, Trans.). New York: Columbia University Press.

Lacan, J. (1977). *Écrits: A selection.* (A. Sheridan, Trans.). London: Tavistock.

Lacan, J. (1992). *The Seminar of Jacques Lacan, Book 7: The ethics of psychoanalysis, 1959–1960.* (D. Porter, Trans.). New York: W.W. Norton.

Lacan, J. (1999). *The Seminar of Jacques Lacan, Book 20: On feminine sexuality, the limits of love and knowledge, 1972–1973.* (B. Fink, Trans.). New York: W.W. Norton.

Lacan, J. (2002). *The Seminar of Jacques Lacan, Book 15: The Psychoanalytic Act, 1967–1968.* (C. Gallagher, Trans.). London: Karnac Books.

Lacan, J. (2005). *The Seminar of Jacques Lacan, Book 23: Le Sinthome, 1975–1976.* Paris: Seuil.

Laplanche, J. (1999). *Essays on otherness.* New York: Routledge.

Lear, J. (2006). *Radical hope: Ethics in the face of cultural devastation.* Cambridge: Harvard University Press.

Levy, J. (2011). The dream in beyond the pleasure principle and beyond. In S. Akhtar & M. K. O'Neil (Eds.), *On Freud's "Beyond the pleasure principle"* (pp.128–153). London: Karnac Books.

Lustiger-Thaler, H. (2010). When empty is full. In *Anish Kapoor: Memory* (pp. 16–19). New York: Guggenheim Museum Publication.

Lyotard, J. F. (2011). *Discourse, figure.* (A. Hudek & M. Lydon, Trans.). Minneapolis, MN: University of Minnesota Press.

Meltzer, D., & Williams, M. H. (2008). *The apprehension of beauty: The role of aesthetic conflict in development, art, and violence.* London: Karnac Books.

Millot, C. (1990). *Horsexe: Essay on transsexuality.* (K. Hylton, Trans.). Brooklyn, NY: Autonomedia.

Nixon, M., & Bourgeois, L. (2005). *Fantastic reality: Louise Bourgeois and the story of modern art.* Cambridge, MA: MIT Press.

Nusselder, A. (2013). *The surface effect: The screen of fantasy in psychoanalysis.* New York: Routledge.

Parker, I. (2011). *Lacanian psychoanalysis: Revolution in subjectivity.* New York: Routledge.

Perelberg, R. J. (2008). *Time, space and phantasy.* New York: Routledge.

Phillips, A. (2013). *Missing out: In praise of the unlived life.* New York: Farrar, Straus and Giroux.

Pluth, E. (2007). *Signifiers and acts: Freedom in Lacan's theory of the subject.* Albany, NY: State University of New York Press.

Poddar, S. (2010). Suspending disbelief: Anish Kapoor's mental sculpture. In *Anish Kapoor: Memory* (pp. 26–53). New York: Guggenheim Museum Publication.

Proust, M. (2001). *In search of lost time.* (C. K. Scott Moncrieff & T. Kilmartin, Trans.). London: Folio Society.

Rilke, R. M. (1999). *The essential Rilke.* (G. Kinnel, & H. Lieberman, Eds. & Trans.). New York: HarperCollins Publishers.

Santner, E. (2005). Miracles happen: Benjamin, Rosenzweig, Freud, and the matter of the neighbor. In *The neighbor: Three inquiries in political theology* (pp. 76–133). Chicago: The University of Chicago Press.

Spivak, G. C. (2010). Signs and trace. In *Anish Kapoor: Memory* (pp. 56–75). New York: Guggenheim Museum Publication.

Verhaeghe, P. (1999). *Does the woman exist? From Freud's hysteric to Lacan's feminine.* (M. du Ry, Trans.). New York: Other Press.

Verhaeghe, P. (2001). *Beyond gender: From subject to drive.* New York: Other Press.

Verhaeghe, P. (2009). *New studies of old villains: A radical consideration of the Oedipus complex.* New York: Other Press.

Winnicott, D. W. (1971). *Playing and reality.* London: Routledge.

Wolff-Bernstein, J. (2011). A matter of choice. [Review of the book *Please Select Your Gender*]. *DIVISION/Review, 3,* 4–5.

Žižek, S. (2002). The Real of sexual difference. In S. Barnard, & B. Fink (Eds.), *Reading Seminar XX: Lacan's major work on love, knowledge, and feminine sexuality* (pp. 57–76). New York: SUNY Press.

Index

abandonment 34–6, 68
absence: aesthetic crisis 7–9; aesthetics 15, 20, 25, 85–6, 91; analytic listening 3; binary model 11; narratives 33; real time 62, 66, 68–9, 71; surgery 48–9, 50, 52, 56; temporality 74–6; thinking and memory 87
Adams, M. 65
Adams, P. 48
adolescence 30, 31–7, 37–8, 38–9, 43–5
aesthetic conflict: narratives 42; states of mind 3–4, 4–5; transitioning 16, 18, 21, 21–2, 25, 29
aesthetic crises 7–14, 16
aesthetics 15–18, 18–20, 21–3, 23–6, 26–9, 85–6
ambiguity: aesthetics 20, 23, 29, 74, 75; dream interpretation 83; narratives 35, 37, 40–1; real time 70; states of mind 6; surgery 47; thinking and memory 87
Ambrosio, G. 9
analytic encounters 3, 21–3, 29, 63, 70
analytic listening 3
analytic objects 17, 31, 91
analytic process: conceptual shifts 87, 89; death and creativity 69–70; ethics 92; narratives 27, 31, 71, 93; surgery 48, 53, 56; transitioning 23
analytic space 59, 61, 88
analytic time 63–4, 65, 69
androgyneity 43
aporia 8, 12, 17, 21–2, 88, 95
Aron (case study) 52–4, 57
art 15–18, 18–20, 21–3, 23–6, 26–9, 85–6
atemporality 65, 69 *see also* temporality

Bass, A.: aesthetics 21–2; sexual difference 84, 85; states of mind 8, 12–13; temporality 63, 64, 65

Benjamin, J. 11
Beyond the Pleasure Principle (Freud) 21, 63, 83
Bhabha, H. 74–6, 86, 90–2
binary gender model 1, 11, 13, 20, 74
Bollas, C. 65
Britzman, D. P. 14, 20, 41, 45, 48, 85
Butler, J. 11–12

Calliope/Cal (case study): enigma of gender 94, 95–6; narratives 30, 31, 32–6, 39–40, 40–1, 46; psychic space 90
case studies *see* Aron; Calliope/Cal; Henry; *Herculine Barbin* (Foucault); Linda; S; Sam; Schreber
cathexis 13
clinical vignettes *see* Aron; Calliope/Cal; Henry; *Herculine Barbin* (Foucault); Linda; S; Sam; Schreber
constructivism 11–12
Copjec, J. 24–5
cross identification 60–2
Crow Nation 2, 77–8, 79–80, 87, 88, 94

de-idealization 22, 41, 71
Dean, T. 11–12, 17, 88
death drive 23–5, 42–3, 70
dedifferentiation 29, 66, 71 *see also* differentiation
Derbyshire, P. 93
Derrida, J. 4, 13, 21
differentiation 13, 25, 65 *see also* dedifferentiation
Does the Woman Exist? (Verhaeghe) 67
doxa 34, 81

Eigen, M. 56
electrolysis 59, 60
embodied apprehension 4–7

embodiment *see* gender embodiment
engenderment: analytical space 87; creation 76, 86, 95; real time 62, 69; transitioning 25–6, 27
enigma of embodiment 19
enigma of gender 35, 36, 38, 73, 86, 92
enigmatic art objects: aesthetics 17, 23; conceptual shifts 73, 76; perceptions 92, 96; states of mind 14
enigmatic objects: aesthetics 15, 18; conceptual shifts 74, 81, 86; and gender 95–6; states of mind 3, 5, 8
enigmatic signifiers 14, 17, 78
essentialism 11, 55, 90
Ettinger, B. 55–6
Eugenides, J. 30, 32–4, 36, 39, 46

feminine jouissance 66–8
feminine jouissance (Verhaeghe) *see also* jouissance
femininity: aesthetics 22; conceptual shifts 83, 87, 88; real time 58, 58–61, 63–4, 65–6, 66–8, 69–72; states of mind 6, 13; surgery 48–9, 52, 56
fetishism: aesthetic crisis 7–9, 14; aesthetics 20, 24, 25; narratives 43; surgery 47
Fort/Da game: conceptual shifts 80–1, 85; narratives 41–3; surgery 47, 53; transitioning 23, 27–9
Foucault, M. 30, 31–2, 34–5
Freud, S.: aesthetics 21–3; conceptual shifts 80–1, 83–4; narratives 32, 34, 42; phantasy and reality 94; states of mind 7–8; surgery 47, 48; temporality 63, 69; transitioning 12, 24, 29

Gasché, R. 83
gender certainty 1, 6, 9, 11, 14, 23
gender embodiment 91–2; conceptual shifts 73, 85–6; conclusions 88; narratives 30, 36, 40–1, 43–4; real time 59–60, 68; states of mind 2, 4–7, 10–14; surgery 47, 53; transitioning 19–20, 23–4, 26–8
gender identity: conceptual shifts 73, 75, 78, 81, 89; narratives 31, 39–40; oscillations 61–2, 63–4, 67–8, 92; states of mind 9–10, 12–13; transitioning 20, 23, 25
gender position 33
gender resignifications 6, 20, 28, 83

genitalia: aesthetics 18; conceptual shifts 66, 73, 93; narratives 31, 33; surgery 53, 54–5
Gherovici, P. 1, 9, 13, 47, 49–51, 52
Green, A. 48, 63

"Hanging Phallus" (Bourgeois artwork) 19–20
Harris, A. 11
Heidegger, M. 4
Henry (case study) 50
Herculine Barbin (Foucault): conclusions 95; narratives 30–1, 31–7, 37–8, 38–40, 42, 45–6
heteronormative ideologies 9–10, 12
hormone therapy 51, 59, 60
hysteria 48, 48–9, 49–50, 66–8

idealization: conceptual shifts 73, 88; femininity 71; narratives 38–9, 41, 45; states of mind 4; surgery 47; transitioning 20, 22, 26, 27
idealized phantasies 57
imaginary constructions 7, 20, 27, 28
imaginary of gender 20, 23, 26, 79, 81, 93
incest 33, 41, 55–6
indeterminacy 2, 36, 86, 88
infantile sexuality 8, 22
interpellations 5, 12, 36, 87, 89
intersex 30–1, 31–4, 39, 44

jouissance: aesthetics 18, 25; conclusions 93–4; femininity 65–6, 66–8; narratives 35, 38; surgery 49, 50–1, 52, 56

Kapoor, A.: aesthetics 15–17, 18–20, 26–7, 85–6; materiality and temporality 74–5, 90–1; states of mind 7
Kristeva, J. 37–8, 42–3, 61, 68–9, 70–1

Lacan. J.: conceptual shifts 85, 93–4; femininity 65–6; narratives 42; states of mind 2–3, 6, 10, 12; surgery 49–52; transitioning 15, 23
Laplanche, J. 8
laws: conceptual shifts 77, 83; narratives 31–2, 37; states of mind 2, 9, 10; surgery 50 *see also* legitimacy
Lear, J. 76–8, 79–80, 81–3, 88, 89
legitimacy 13, 32
Levy, J. 83–4
Linda (case study) 51

literature 30–46; adolescence 31–7, 37–8; analytic objects 30–1; embodiment 38–40; rewriting the narrative 40–3, 43–6; surgery 47, 49
Lustiger-Thaler, H. 15–16
Lyotard, J. F. 90–1

masculine image 58, 59
masculinity: conceptual shifts 83, 87, 88; real time 59–60, 60–1, 63–4, 68, 69–71; states of mind 6, 13; surgery 48–9, 52, 53–4, 56, 57; transitioning 22
maternal body 3, 6, 18
maternal discourse 51, 62, 68
maternal engulfment 65–6
maternal figures 34–5, 42, 67
maternal Other 70
maternal phallus 7–8
matricide 68–9
meaninglessness 16, 19, 51, 54, 55–6
Meltzer, D. 3–4, 4–5, 18, 22
memoirs 30, 31–7, 38–9, 51
"Memory" (Kapoor installation) 7, 15–17, 18, 20, 26–7
Middlesex (Eugenides) 30, 32–4, 39, 40, 45–6

necrotizing tendencies 6, 10, 41
negations 46, 70, 87, 91
normative "real" 64
normative sexuality 8
Nusselder, A. 76

Oedipal story 33, 48–9

paradigms 7, 9, 22, 78, 80
paradoxes: conceptual shifts 79, 80, 82, 87, 89; narratives 32, 34, 35, 44–5; real time 68–9, 70; states of mind 4–5, 10, 12; surgery 50, 52; transitioning 17, 21, 24–5, 28–9
pathological conditions 1, 9, 11
penis: S (case study) 59; states of mind 7–8, 11; surgery 48, 50, 53; transitioning 19–20, 22, 25
phallic monism (non-castrated/castrated) 8
phantasized Other, 30, 54
phantasms 44, 45, 50, 55–6, 90
phantasy of rebirth 47
Phillips, A. 36
Please Select Your Gender (Gherovici) 47

Plenty Coups (Chief of the Crow Nation) 77–8, 79–80, 81–3, 86–7, 94
Pluth, E. 27–8, 46, 49, 50–2, 81, 85
Poddar, S. 16–17, 26–7
polymorphous perversity: aesthetics 17, 20, 21, 22, 24, 28; conceptual shifts 73, 86; conclusions 94; narratives 32, 37, 43; states of mind 5, 7, 8, 12; surgery 54–5
primal encounters 18–20
primary narcissism 4, 12–13
prohibitions: conceptual shifts 87; femininity 67, 70; gender oscillation 63; narratives 33, 39–40; surgery 55–6
Proust, M. 26, 28, 42–3, 45
psychic death 60–2
psychic identification 2
psychic positions: conceptual shifts 79; real time 61, 68, 71; states of mind 1, 4, 6, 8, 10; transitioning 21, 28
psychic space: conclusions 90, 92; real time 64; states of mind 4, 10; transitioning 18, 20, 21–3, 25
psychoanalytic discourse 9, 10, 13–14, 23, 32
psychoanalytic narratives 27, 31, 71, 93

Radical Hope (Lear) 77–8, 79
re-birth 7, 33–4, 36, 46
resignifications 6, 20, 28, 83

S (case study) 58–60, 60–2, 62–5, 65–6, 66–8, 69–72
Sam (case study) 43–5, 87, 89, 94
Santner, E. 17
Schreber (case study) 50
self-injury 2
sex change 55
sex reassignment surgery (SRS) 7, 28, 47, 53, 88–9, 92–3
sexual difference: conceptual shifts 74, 79, 81–3; narratives 46, 50, 52; real time 65–6, 68–9; states of mind 1–2, 5–7, 8–14; surgery 54–7; transitioning 20–2, 26
sexual embodiment 2, 11, 13, 23
sexual identification 7–10, 22–4, 66
sinthome 49–52, 56
SRS (sex reassignment surgery) 7, 28, 47, 53, 88–9, 92–3
sublimation 4, 23–6, 26–9, 42, 45

Index

surgery 47–57; aesthetics 18, 28; conceptual shifts 89; conclusions 92–5; identification 48–9, 52–4; novel beginning 54–7; sinthome 49–52; states of mind 7
symbolic construction 74, 79

temporality: conceptual shifts 74–6, 78, 80–1, 88; narratives 46; real time 65–6, 69; surgery 56; transitioning 15, 29
time in the primary 62–5
transference: conceptual shifts 84; conclusions 96; narratives 32, 42–3, 44–5; real time 62, 70; states of mind 10; surgery 47; transitioning 16, 28–9
transgressions: narratives 32, 33, 35, 37, 40; real time 68, 70; states of mind 2, 10; surgery 56
transitional objects 8, 25, 31, 79
transitional phenomena 65
transitionality: aesthetics 16, 22, 24, 28; conceptual shifts 73–5, 80, 89; narratives 40; real time 61, 66, 69–70; states of mind 4, 5, 6
transsexual body: conceptual shifts 73–4, 86, 88; conclusions 91–2; states of mind 4–5, 7, 13–14; surgery 51, 53–4, 55, 56; transitioning 15, 17, 26, 27
transsexual discourse 45
transsexual dream interpretation 83–5
transsexual patients 1–2, 9–10, 34, 50, 88
traumatic dreams 84
traumatic Real (Verhaeghe) 6, 66, 73

vagina 19, 25
Verhaeghe, P. 48, 61, 67
violation of boundaries 3, 34
"Void" (Kapoor installation) 91

Winnicott, D. W. 4, 6–7, 9, 61, 65–6, 69
Wolff-Bernstein, J. 9

Žižek, S. 5